Contents

Preface

This book on career development in business, industry, and government organizations came out of my twenty years of work as an internal and external career development consultant in organizations. As an external consultant, I was called on to design career development programs for specific organizations because there was not a readily available handbook or skill-building seminar that the organization's human resources staff could turn to in order to design and build their own customized program. True, a few expensive workshops were held at large universities each year that had "career development" in the title. But most of these were heavy on theory, short on practical application, and devoid of specific skill-building practice. And there have been a few publications that addressed organizational career development. Some were general and superficial. Some just reported the results of surveys of organizations in general terms. Others highlighted (and promoted) only programs in organizations that were clients of the authors. All were written by academics who knew more about research and writing than they did about the world of the worker and the manager. This book is written at the request of hundreds of human resource managers, career counselors, and organizational development consultants who have attended my workshops and seminars on career development in organizations. These practitioners have asked for a practical handbook that they and their peers can use to develop effective career coaching programs that will maximize the career potential of all employees and meet the business needs of the organizations.

This book is not just a "cookbook" of practical how-to checklists for career development. It has an overview of some basic models and theories of career development. To make these models less academic and theoretical, I have included simple diagrams and expanded these diagrams with examples of real people developing their careers in real organizations. I have incorporated some assessment instruments and some forms for focusing on career goals and writing personal career strategy plans. My orientation toward learning is to engage the reader in an interactive process. Consequently, I am offering each reader the opportunity to take and score the assessment instruments, actively engage in some of the recommended career exploration field research activities, form career goals or mission statements, and, finally, to develop a career action plan. By actively applying the career development process to yourself rather than passively receiving information, you will obtain not only an intellectual understanding of career development, but an emotional or personal awareness of the process. When you do work with your employees, you will be using a process that has worked for you and that you are really comfortable with.

The process in this book works with employees in all types of organizations—city governments, profit-making private organizations, social service agencies, or universities. These organizations all have employees. The managers of these organizations face similar issues. While acknowledging the unique differences between individuals, I have introduced a basic career development model, as well as career assessment, research, and planning tools, that will be effective with employees at all levels, in all occupations, and in all types of organizations.

Now a little about my background. I am a professional career counselor with a master's degree in counseling psychology. My academic training came fairly late in life. I spent fifteen years in business and industry doing a variety of jobs before I started college. I started working in 1971 as a guidance consultant, training professional school and college counselors in the career counseling and career development process. In the mid-1970s, I took on an assignment at Lawrence Livermore National Laboratory to install and develop several programs, including a career development program for all employees. By the late 1970s, I was consulting to other organizations on career development issues and conducting seminars on career development techniques for counselors, trainers, and human resources professionals throughout the United States. During the 1980s, I established and operated an executive outplacement firm in California's Silicon Valley. Most recently I have been spending time teaching career coaching techniques to frontline managers and human resource professionals throughout the United States, the Pacific Rim, and Europe.

Overview of Career Development in Organizations

Career development in organizations today is not the same thing that it was fifteen or twenty years ago—or even ten years ago. Let me take you briefly through the historical evolution of career development in organizations.

The Individual Model

The very first types of career development programs fall into what I call the *individual* model (see figure 1). They were generally based on motivation theory and focused on moving toward self-actualization. They were a device for growth and development of the individual and were very much driven by the individual.

Some of these programs were started by the National Training Labs (NTL) in the late 1960s and early 1970s. Employees

Figure 1   The Individual Model of Career Development

volunteered for these training programs, which frequently involved
off-site activities such as a two-week retreat. The organization
knew little about the content or process, and their main role was to
pay the bills. The programs focused on individual development and
the search for self-actualization, and they were often organized and
led by counseling psychologists who admired the works of Maslow.
Many of the career development techniques and activities from
these early programs were popularized by Richard Bolles in his
classic book, *What Color Is Your Parachute?*

Employees who participated in these individual programs
reported feeling renewed and revitalized and frequently had a
clearer vision of mission and purpose. But they frequently could
not verbalize any direct, measurable relationship between the activity and their job. More importantly, the management of the organization could trace no clear positive effect of the program on the
organization's bottom line.

The Organizational Model

An *organizational* or *career pathing* model of career development
deals with identifying career paths (see figure 2). These programs
evolved in the mid-1970s and focused on fast-track employees.
They sometimes involved assessment centers and were very much
management driven. In these organizational models, there was

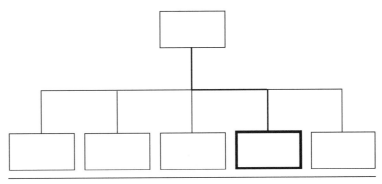

Figure 2   The Organizational Model of Career Development

more accountability than in the very individual models, where an employee might decide to quit being an accountant and become a Buddhist monk! These career-pathing programs were particularly popular with the federal government.

The assessment center technology (e.g., some of the work of Chabot Jaffe, Developmental Dimensions International, and Assessment Designs) that was often used in the career-pathing programs grew out of AT&T's work in the late 1960s and early 1970s. In an assessment center, trained managers put employees through simulated managerial activities and measured them to see how well they performed. Sometimes these programs were called career development programs, and in all cases, they were management driven and designed strictly for the benefit of the organization: Management decided who would be involved in the programs, designed the programs, and controlled how people went through them.

Many of the organizations that set these programs up for fast-track employees created a kind of "caste system" within the organization. Someone might say, "Well, this person's a fast-tracker, let's give her these extra activities and send her through." This could be very threatening to other employees and created some obvious problems.

Sometimes favoritism was involved. Occasionally management would identify fast-track people and try to develop their potential without telling them, and they were really astounded when those people quit their jobs. So some of these programs were fairly disastrous.

The Partnership Model

Let's move to the model that I think came out of the 1970s and took us into the 1980s, which I will call the *partnership* model (see figure 3). In the partnership model, the different needs and roles of the players were really addressed: The organization provided the resources for career development, the supervisor provided the counseling and coaching, and the employee provided the direction and motivation. So we have three different players playing different roles, but they do it together in a cooperative method.

A New Model for Career Development

We have seen that in the early programs there was a realization that in order for a program to really take off, in terms of the individual, the individual had to drive it. On the other hand, the person that we tended to leave out of programs in the early 1970s was the supervisor, who had no role in the counseling process—we brought outsiders in to do that. Yet the supervisor and the manager are the ones who really need to be involved in career coaching, not the HR people who don't get to know the employees like a manager does. The manager should be providing some coaching. So we saw a tremendous effort in the early 1980s to move in the direction of the manager providing the coaching, and the organization providing the resources. The organization hired the people to do the training and provided the books, materials, tests, and the training room. So,

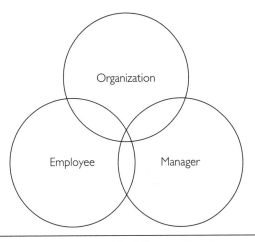

Figure 3   The Partnership Model of Career Development

we evolved from the individual orientation to the organizational model to the partnership model. I think that it is still fairly prominent right now, but we currently seem to be evolving further toward yet another new model. This new model, which is presented in table 1, is actually a culmination of all of these models. It includes the partnership function, but it is also viewed as running across the entire organization. This model can be used in the following ways:

- As a succession planning tool
- As a tool to help the organization do long-range planning in terms of resource planning for the organization
- As a tool for promoting an integrated system for middle management in the organization
- As a motivation tool for supervisors
- As a tool for mobility

In the remainder of this book, we will discuss the four stages of career development that are presented in table 2 within the context of the nine steps needed for effective implementation of career development in organizations.

Table I New Model for Career Development

Manager's Role and Responsibility	Employee's Career Development Activities	Human Resources' Support Structure
The Coach	*The Driver*	*The Support System*
Assessor • Assesses and identifies skills, interests, and motivations • Gives feedback on observed behaviors and exhibited skills	*Assessment* • Technical skills • Transferable skills • Career values • Occupational interests • Work or management style	Employee orientation Coach training class Career development center
Information provider • Informs employee about options and barriers • Gives employee printed information	*Exploration of options* • Promotion (moving up) • Enrichment (adding tasks) • Entrenchment (staying put) • Transfer (moving out) • Rotation (moving around) • Resigning (moving out)	Individual career counseling Performance appraisal system
Referral agent • Refers employee to people who can be of assistance • Refers employee to books and other types of information	*Career focus* • Specific goal • Clear goal • Compatible goal • Available goal • Appropriate goal • *What* is the specific goal? • *Why* is this the best goal? (evidence of appropriateness)	Career development workshops Job posting system Job descriptions
Guide • Encourages employee to focus on an available goal • Gives employee reality feedback on the appropriateness of the goal		Job family system Career path system EEO/Affirmative action
Teacher • Tutors the employee in writing the career strategy plan • Encourages employee through steps of the development plan • Encourages employee to implement the career plan	*Career strategy plan* • *How* will goal be pursued? (Outline specific steps.) • *When* will each step occur? (Develop a time line of steps.) • *Who* else is involved? (people who can help; people the plan will affect)	Internal training programs Succession planning program Tuition reimbursement program
Developer • Assigns employee to developmental roles and tasks • Promotes employee when readiness is demonstrated		Supervisory/ Management development program

Table 2   The Four Stages of Career Development

Stage 1 *Assessment*	What are my skills, values, interests, and work style?
Stage 2 *Exploration*	What options do I have?
Stage 3 *Goal Setting* *and Planning*	Which option is the best possible option for me, i.e., my goal? • Why is this the best goal for me?
Stage 4 *Strategy*	How will I get to my goal? • What specific behaviors will I engage in to get there? • When will each step occur? • Who else is involved or needs to be involved?

Define Career Development in the Organization

The first of the nine steps to building a successful career development program for an organization begin with defining career development and specifying exactly who career development is for. For too many employees and managers, career development has been just a vague concept that everyone accepts as important but nobody can really define. In Step 1, we will describe the elements of career development.

Career Decision Making Is a Process, Not an Event

Career decision making is no longer a once-in-a-lifetime event. In 1950, at the midpoint of the twentieth century, planning, acquiring, and maintaining a career was very much like riding a train. When you decided where you wanted to go, you purchased a ticket, boarded the train at the gate with the sign for your destination, and rode steadily along the fixed and stable tracks until the train reached your destination. There were no detours, no changes in the route, you just sat back and relaxed while the engineer, conductor, and crew took you where you wanted to go.

In 1950 I was a plumber's helper. I had boarded the "plumbing train" and I was positive that I would move from plumber's helper to apprentice plumber, journeyman plumber, foreman plumber, master plumber, and maybe plumbing contractor. The nature of the job wouldn't change. The career path wouldn't change. My career route was as predictable as the train route. And that was the way almost everyone in 1950 viewed careers and jobs. And that view was accurate for many people in the 1950s. Riding a train was an appropriate metaphor for the way people viewed careers and jobs in the 1950s, but it had become obsolete by the 1960s and 1970s.

In 1970 we needed a new metaphor to describe the dynamics of career and job decision making. Career decision making became more like riding a bus. When you boarded the bus for your destination each day, you didn't get on a vehicle that operated on fixed and stable tracks. With the bus, you were on a vehicle that could change its route when the road conditions and traffic patterns changed. You were now on a vehicle that could even change its ultimate destination. You could even transfer or change buses in midroute if you desired.

Career decision making in the 1970s became much more flexible, allowing the occupation to change with the technology and economy and permitting the individual to make mid-career changes. But, as with the train, we still relied on the bus company to set the schedule and route while we just sat back and let them do the driving. Now we need a new metaphor that will describe career planning and decision making for the new century.

To successfully navigate the career and job world of the twenty-first century, we need to move to the *sports utility vehicle* as our metaphor for career planning. The sports utility vehicle is flexible and fast. It does not require fixed transit schedules or even paved roads. Routes can be changed or modified every year, month, week, day, hour, or even minute. And the individual is in the driver's seat.

The careers in the twenty-first century will not be steady and fixed. The computer technology of the 1950s and 1960s brought us thousands of keypunch operator jobs—but today's computer technology has now eliminated all of these jobs. A combination of an emerging technology and changing social habits has now replaced many bank teller positions with automatic teller machines. We can't predict the specific jobs that will emerge in the twenty-first century, but what we do know with a high degree of certainty is that those employees who have learned to drive their own careers will be able to prepare for, acquire, and master the careers and jobs that emerge.

The first goal of this book is to show you how to inspire employees to take control of their careers and to steer and drive those careers toward attaining their own personal satisfaction.

Career Development Is Possible During Rolling Recessions and Bad Times

At a Stanford University conference several years ago, economist and futurist Richard Carlson predicted that the recessions and downsizings of the late 1980s were not a temporary economic anomaly but rather a pattern of regular fluctuations that will be with us for the predictable future. Management training programs routinely included how to deal with layoffs and downsizings as part of their curriculum. Even the most healthy of companies have learned to plan to contract as well as expand their workforce.

Career Development Can Exist
in a Two-Tiered Workforce

Not many years ago companies advertised "temporary" and "permanent" positions. No more! Corporate counselors are careful to advise their clients that if they tell an employee a job is "permanent" they could face a lawsuit if they try to terminate that employee from that job. So now we have two distinct types of workers: *regular* or *core* employees, who will hold the jobs as long as they perform satisfactorily and as long as the company needs them; and the *temporary* or *contingent* employees who are hired for a specific project or assignment and can expect to be terminated or reassigned at the conclusion of the project. The general expectation of most corporations is that much of the regular workforce will be retained during recessions and downsizings, while the temporary or contingent employees will be the first to go.

There are pluses and minuses to this two-tiered workforce. On the positive side, there are many contract and part-time jobs available for those workers who choose not to commit themselves to a long-term relationship with an organization because they value the freedom and independence of being able to move on to new challenges and environments. On the negative side, many of these jobs do not pay as well as the so-called regular jobs. More importantly, we are facing the dilemma of having created a category of second-class workers—an underclass who is paid less, has fewer benefits, and performs the less-desirable tasks on the job. The two-tiered workforce is here for now. The question is, Where are we going with this new phenomenon?

Career Development Can Coexist
With the Delayering of Middle Management

As the twentieth century comes to a close, most successful companies (and some government agencies) are eliminating several layers of redundant middle management. Peter Drucker has predicted

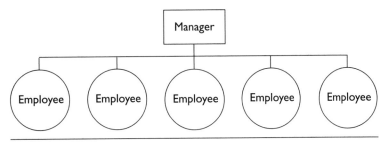

Figure 4a Old Managerial Model

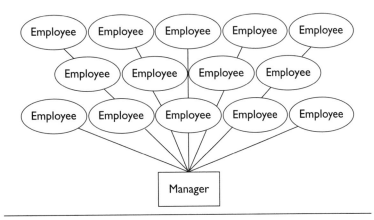

Figure 4b New Managerial Model

that the organization of the future will look much less like the hierarchical military chain-of-command and more like the symphony orchestra (see figures 4a and 4b). Decision-making authority will be moved down in the organization, and the span of control and authority of any manager will be greatly enlarged. The new manager will not be expected to be a technical expert who will teach and monitor the workers very closely. He or she will perform more like the symphony conductor who facilitates the actions of dozens of musicians, who know their instruments better than the conductor, in order to create a product that none of them could have created on their own.

For this new model of management to work, it is imperative not only for management to loosen control from the top, but for employees to become empowered and take control of their individual careers. The four-stage career development model articulated in this publication is the foundation that employees can use to gain control. The nine steps outlined in this book can be used by organizations to build an effective employee career development program.

Career Development Is Possible Even With the New Work Options

In the last several years, organizations in this country have begun to restructure where and how they get their work done. *Job sharing,* in which two part-time workers share a single position or assignment, has been instituted in many companies. *Flextime,* in which the start or finishing time is modified from the traditional nine-to-five pattern, has been successful in numerous organizations. *Telecommuting,* in which employees work from home or another site, has quickly gained in popularity.

Organizations traditionally have been slow to respond to any of these new work options when they have been considered at the request of employees—for example, when a working parent asks to schedule her work time around her children's school schedule. However, many organizations have now learned that to remain competitive and attract and retain their most valued employees and to keep pace with the influence of technology and its requirements, they must adopt new work options on an ongoing basis.

Career Development May Not Be Possible for Low-Skill Jobs With Low Pay

The willingness to "just work hard" used to be the ticket to success in this country. But nearly every job in the twenty-first century will require technology skills. It was not long ago when the only people who were expected to understand and use computers, for example, were computer programmers. But times have changed. Just ride in any big-city taxicab and you can observe the driver entering data about the number of passengers and their destination in a dashboard computer. Check your baggage at the airport curb, and the skycap enters your name into the computer and your personalized baggage tags are instantly produced. You will even find a computer in the cab of a tractor cultivating a wheat field in Kansas. We have moved swiftly toward a society of high-skilled "haves" and low-skilled "have nots," and we have some choice about which group we belong to.

Career Development Will Favor
the Knowledge Worker

Gone are the days when the young entry-level worker with little education went to work for a company, learned and mastered that company's product, and lived happily ever after. Overspecialization without a broad foundation of knowledge can lead to obsolescence. Security for the knowledge worker (if there is such a thing anymore as security) rests not in the mastery of a specific job at a specific organization, but in the personal development of a body of knowledge and skills that is transportable across organizations and occupations.

A case in point is that of the "Lockheed engineers," a generic term for overspecialized engineers at any number of aerospace companies, who flourished before the aerospace downsizings of the late 1960s and early 1970s. The "Lockheed engineers" joined the organization in boom times with little education and no experience. They were quick learners and hard workers and quickly became experts. But they were narrow experts who maybe knew virtually everything about the base of the rear antenna on the L-2 rocket-powered satellite, but very little else about engineering. They were very valuable employees while that particular product was being built—but, unfortunately, also very expendable when the company moved on to a new product line.

Career Development Is Really
in the Eye of the Beholder

The way that we view career development depends on our position in the organization and our experience in the world of work. In organizational career development, it is very important that both the employees (the program users), the human resources staff (the teachers) and all levels of management (the sponsors) share a similar definition of career development. I have frequently been disappointed when I've looked at books that were advertised as being about career development and found them to be about job change, job search, job rotation, job enrichment, or career paths—all of which can be *aspects* of career development, but none of which is career development by itself.

The Employee's View of Career Development

When I started doing career development in organizations twenty years ago, the first view of career development that I was exposed to was that of employees at the bottom of the organizational pyramid (see figure 5). Being at the bottom of the pyramid, the only direction the employee can look is up. When we talked about career development, they heard "These are the career paths." "This is how you move up." "These are the skills you will need to move up in these paths." "This is where you can get training to move up." "This is how long will it take you to move up." In their minds, career development equals *upward mobility*.

In most of today's organizations, we don't have the traditional pyramidal structure anymore. Organizations have flattened out. The time is long past when a large segment of the employee population just waits for a higher-level job to open up. Even if organizations still looked like pyramids, we would still have a lot of impaction, plateauing, stagnation, or attrition because there is clearly not enough room at the top for everybody to move up. As

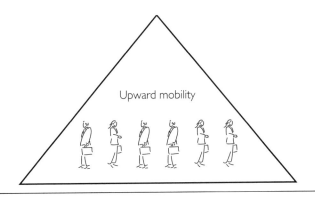

Figure 5   Employee's View of Career Development

career counselors or human resources professionals, when we hang out our career development shingles, employees will view that shingle differently than we do. The employee will read "Promotions and Upward Mobility Offered Here." As professional career counselors, we tend to think of career development in terms of a process that requires hard work and discipline and involves assessment techniques, exploratory research, goal setting, planning activities, and continuing education. But, that is *our view;* career development professionals must deal with the reality of the *employee's view* as well.

The Supervisor's View of Career Development

A second view of career development is that of supervisors or first-level managers. They are closer to the center of the organizational pyramid, and view career development differently than the employee does (see figure 6). When the supervisors hear "career development," they think, How can I motivate my employees? How can I work to coach my employees? What can I do to keep good workers? How can I get rid of the poor performers? Is there some class that I can take to learn how to motivate my employees? To the supervisor, career development equals *motivation and retention.*

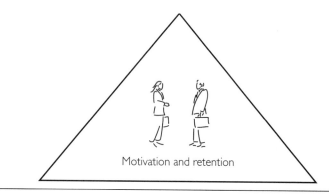

Motivation and retention

Figure 6   Supervisor's View of Career Development

When career development professionals start working with supervisors and first-line managers in organizations, the supervisors really aren't thinking about upward mobility. They're thinking:

> I've got these very real problems right now: I've got these employees I'm trying to motivate. I've got some good employees that I certainly don't want to lose. This career development stuff might mean that HR is trying to move good people out of my department. I don't want that to occur. What do you mean, you people from HR want to do career development? I'm the one that's responsible for career development in my troops because I work with them every day. So you just give me some tools I can use, and I want the tools right now because I have an employee I want to use them with right after lunch.

Allow me to relate a personal anecdote about the supervisor's view of career development. About twenty years ago, I was giving a career development workshop for employees in an organization where I worked as an internal consultant. One of the participants in the workshop that I was leading was my secretary, Laura, who happened to be in the process of typing the final draft of the paper that I was going to present at an international conference on career development the following week. Laura was listening intently as I was presenting an important segment of the career development workshop. Abruptly, in the middle of delivering this segment, a little voice inside said, "Why doesn't Laura go back to the office and finish typing the paper, because we really need to get it out?"

This little voice inside really startled me. Then it dawned on me that the voice was not the part of me who is a career counselor and values the long-range results of the class that we were involved in that day. The voice came from the part of me who was a first-level manager responsible for getting the work of the division accomplished on schedule. So the part of me that is a career counselor and a trainer was doing my training, and the part of me that was a first-line manager was being nagged by wanting her to get back to work. Ever since that day, I have really appreciated the dilemma that first-line supervisors have and the stress that they are put under when they look at long-range career development in relation to the immediate job requirements.

Top Management's View of Career Development

Let me move to the next level of the organization, top management, and examine their view of career development. Top management thinks of career development in terms of identifying potential managers or *succession planning* (see figure 7). Their focus is on identifying which employees have the right skills to meet the challenges that the organization will face in coming years. Top management is worrying about how to get employees trained to move into new positions and about determining when those employees will be ready to move. So what happens when I talk to top managers about career development? When I say "career development," they hear "succession planning." And, unlike the first-line supervisor who asks, "What do I need immediately?" the top manager asks, "What do we need to do in the next five to seven years in order to have the right people with the right skill mix in place?"

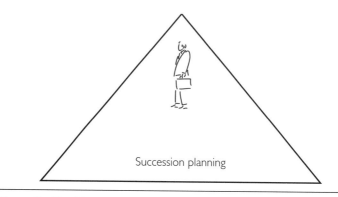

Figure 7   Top Management's View of Career Development

When I first started working with career development in organizations, my interactions were, for the most part, limited to employees. However, shortly after starting to conduct employee career development programs, I was asked to make a presentation to top management. Since I like to be prepared, I got to the executive conference room a few minutes early to check on the overhead projector and other equipment. The only other person there was the organization's president. He introduced himself and said, "I have been looking forward to meeting the person who's going to help us with our succession planning."

Now I'd been around a little bit, so instead of asking, "Excuse me, what is succession planning?" I said, "Yes, I understand that is going to be one of the areas I'll be working on." Then, as soon as I got the opportunity, I got the answer to my question from a colleague. Fortunately, I was able to direct my presentation to the long-range goals and effect of career development activities on the succession and staffing patterns of the organization.

Middle Management's View of Career Development

To supplement these three views of career development, let me introduce a fourth view—that of the middle managers in a large

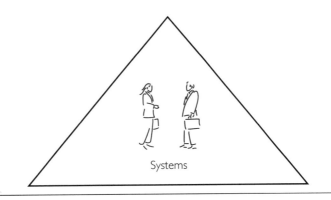

Figure 8   Middle Management's View of Career Development

organization. The middle manager's concerns about career development have to do with the area of *systems* (see figure 8). The questions they are concerned with include:

> How will career development fit with our EEO and affirmative action efforts? How will it relate to our management training, our organizational development systems, our job posting program, the employment function, and the many other functions related to human resources?

So middle managers, who are right in the middle of this organization, really like to view career development as fitting in with all of the other systems. If we listen to middle management and ensure that career development is truly integrated with many of the related human resource functions and programs, we will minimize the negative effects that the now too-frequent economic downturns will have on career development. Over the past ten years, we have seen that career development functions that were instituted in organizations, but not systematically integrated with key human resources functions, have dropped by the wayside. On the other hand, integrated career development programs that are part of the "muscle" of the organization have continued to function.

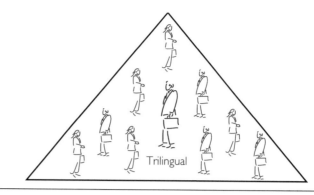

Figure 9   Human Resources' View of Career Development

Human Resources' View of Career Development

The human resources professionals are also right in the middle of the organization and in the middle of the action. They have the employee coming in and asking, "How can I get a promotion? What can I do to get that next job?" They get frequent visits from the first-line supervisor who asks, "What can I do to motivate my employees?" Then top management sends a memo saying, "We need to be thinking about our long-range planning and making sure we identify people's skills so we can fill some slots in the future." The HR person is really stuck right in the middle and has to be "trilingual"—to understand and speak the language of the employees, the supervisor, and top management (see figure 9). And in order to survive, he or she has to do it in a systematic way that fits in with the other parts of the organization.

Summary of Career Development Views Within an Organization

Each person, depending on his or her vantage point within the organization, views career development differently. The employee who is looking at upward mobility wants to move within the next year. The first-level manager or supervisor, who feels an immediate need for assistance, worries about motivation, productivity, and performance. Top management, who takes a long-range view of five to seven years in the future, is focused on the big picture and concerned with the selection and identification of people to move up in the organization.

Ironically, the top management is not really concerned about people moving out as much as lower management is. First-line supervisors are concerned about letting a person leave this week because they have to get production out this week. Top management understands that in order to get the right people in the organization, some people have to move on. Top management is much more receptive than the other sectors to what I call "open" career planning and career development.

Who Are the Consumers of Career Development in Organizations?

While typical career development programs serve a wide variety of clients (i.e., clerical and administrative employees, stagnated midlife professionals, young semiskilled workers, and even high-tech scientists) most organizations that institute career development programs are disproportionately concerned with one particular group of employees—the "young professionals" in that organization.

What Career Development Can Do for Young Professionals

"Young professionals" are the employees who provide the core work in the organization. If the organization is in the high-tech research and development business, then the young professionals are mostly engineers; in a city government, they are the professional planners or administrators who provide key services for the public; in a university, they are the professors and administrators; in a social service agency, they are social workers.

Young professionals in an organization are often asking important questions, such as, "Should I make a move into management?" In almost all organizations, the people who provide the technical work have had no management training while preparing for their career in college. Most engineers that I know have never had a management course while in engineering school. That's one reason why organizations in North America are spending billions of dollars each year on management training for employees. Young professionals often arrive on the job with no knowledge or skills about how to manage.

Young professionals have many concerns about making the move into management. They don't know whether they have appropriate management skills. They are not sure how moving into management will affect their lifestyle. They are not sure whether moving into management will cause them to lose their technical skills. They don't know how to acquire needed managerial skills. Sometimes there is a tremendous amount of pressure from family to move into management for financial reasons. Even in companies like IBM that have dual compensation tracks where individual contributors and managers can make exactly the same amount of money, many young professionals still feel pressured psychologically to move into management. And making the decision to move into management can be even more difficult in academia. When professors become administrators or deans, they often move down—both psychologically and socially.

During the 1980s I was involved in a significant amount of corporate outplacement in California's Silicon Valley. A typical candidate (the person being outplaced) was a vice president or director of engineering, usually a white male in his midthirties who had become head of engineering in the small, but fast-growing, company because he was the best engineer in the company. Unfortunately, he might also have been the worst manager in the company.

I've conducted many exit interviews and I've talked to dozens of personnel generalists who have conducted exit interviews. These exit interviewers have seen too many young engineers offer reasons such as these for leaving the organization: "It's not for more money; I'm leaving because my management is bad" or "My manager is insensitive." Unfortunately, by the time the organization decides to do something about the management problem, it's often too late. The vice president won't take a demotion because he is too ego-invested in the job, so he is terminated and sent to the outplacement counselor.

What has this mismatch cost that organization? Start with $15,000 for the outplacement firm, and even more to have a search firm find a suitable replacement for the vice president of engineering. But the most significant cost can be the loss of the engineers who have left over the years. The costs of having vacant positions, training new employees to get up to speed, and hiring a search firm to find replacements can be significant—not to mention the cost of damaged morale.

A tremendous amount of money could have been saved if a young professional had made a more appropriate career decision several years earlier. An organization can pay for a career development program if it assists just two or three of these people per year to make wise career decisions. Sometimes the wrong decision is to go into management, sometimes it is not to go into management. In most organizations, it is within this group of young professionals that the most visible payoff is going to occur.

What Career Development Can Do for the Clerical Employee

Many administrative assistants, who are in an occupation that is primarily female, are asking, "How can I make more money?" They may work in an organization where lots of people make more money than they do. Hearing that they will need to undertake more education, the next question often is, "How can I balance my family and career?" A typical administrative assistant that career counselors work with is about thirty-two years old, has less than one year in college, has two kids, and may even be the sole support of her family. She is wondering how she can get from being "just an administrative assistant" to being an engineer, or from being an administrative assistant to being an administrator or something in between that narrows the gap. When people need to make a career or job change, they often feel like the acrobat on the flying trapeze. They have to let go of one trapeze before they can grab another one. Many employees need a "bridge job" to get to the other side. All too often for administrative assistants and other clerical employees there are no bridge jobs. Consequently, many are asking, "Where can I get some help to develop my career?"

To illustrate this class of employees, let me talk about some real persons, a number of real administrative assistants I have worked with. These were very competent people, who have spent a number of years in their clerical jobs. Often there is a lot of pressure from society, from others, and from themselves: "You ought to do something other than just being an administrative assistant." (They frequently refer themselves as being "just an administrative assistant.") When one of these administrative assistants visits the local community college and says, "I want to be an engineer, or a public administrator," the community college counselor responds that they have programs to help the administrative assistant train to be an engineer or public administrator and that all the administrative assistant will need to do is register and take courses, and, as a matter of fact, it will only take eight or nine years. And it will involve going to classes Monday, Tuesday, Wednesday, and Thursday nights, and by the way, she will have to study on Friday nights, Saturday, and Sunday too. Consequently, the administrative assistant comes to the organization's career development office and says, "Look, I've got two little kids, and I need to spend some time with them, but I also need to work on my career. What can the organization do for me? Is there some bridge job here for me? How do I get from being a nonexempt to an exempt?" These are tough questions. If you advertise that you are going to do career development, you may have in mind just doing career development with young professionals. When the Career Center sign goes up, you are going to have administrative assistants and other clerical people lining up for services, whether you want them or not.

An effective career development program can assist administrative and clerical employees in a number of ways. An initial learning exercise for most career development program participants is to begin viewing themselves as a portfolio of valuable, transferable skills, rather than go as a job title. Individuals can also be taught to identify areas where "bridge jobs" can be created and learn methods to convince management of the advantages of creating such jobs. They can also learn how to set new goals and create strategic plans.

What Career Development Can Do for the Stagnated Employee

An important potential consumer of organizational career development is the employee that I will call the mature professional. I first encountered this group in large numbers when I worked in an engineering organization in the 1970s. When I first started dealing with them, they were all men, all about age forty, all individual contributors, and all rather shy people and not very verbal. When one of these mature professionals would come to my office he might relate a history like this:

> Twenty years ago, I said I'd be an engineer, a husband, and a father; now I'm all of those. But what else is there for me in life? I'm not really happy with who I am and what I am doing. Why doesn't my boss give me challenging assignments anymore? Do other professionals have any of the same concerns that I have?

This individual feels very isolated and alone and has no idea that there are many other people in the same organization with the same concerns. The age range for these mature professionals has expanded to include people in their fifties, and now maybe fifteen to twenty percent are women.

These are stagnated and burned-out professionals. They are people who were doing an excellent job fifteen to twenty years ago. If we examined their performance appraisals, we would see that they used to exceed requirements but they are now doing just enough to get by. This is a person who has been stagnating for years and moving down in performance. Can you imagine how much money the organization has lost each year that the person moved through those categories? Each year that performance is below potential means a loss for the organization in terms of return on investment. There is also an accompanying loss of self-esteem for the individual. These stagnated professionals don't know where their careers are going or why their bosses don't give them challenging assignments anymore. This particular stage of transition has long been recognized for men, but now it is starting to be predictable for more and more women as well. This is the time in life when people start to question what their goals are, where they are now, where they might go, how much time they have left.

There are very real possibilities for remarkable turnaround with these individuals. Many stagnated individuals have been revitalized through career development programs. There are only two paths to revitalization—the employee can either start contributing within the organization or move out to a new organization. The result of either path is a win-win situation: If they leave, the organization will put somebody else in their position who is a better fit; and if they stay, their productivity and effectiveness increases. If a stagnated employee wants to stay with the organization, they usually need the active cooperation of their manager. It is difficult for stagnated employees to move back to productivity by themselves.

How do some employees get stagnated? In many instances this is a person who has chosen to stay an individual contributor rather than move into management. They may have done so unconsciously or consciously, but they are paying the price for that now.

In other cases the good intentions of the organization have contributed to the situation. For example, I worked with one organization that hired many professionals right out of college. The organization paid them good money and gave them good benefits and interesting work to do. About fifteen years down the line, the work of the organization changed radically, and many highly specialized professionals became obsolete. The work of the organization didn't require their skills anymore. These employees had given control of their careers over to an organization that had treated them very well, but unfortunately, the organization had to lay them off. The company felt a tremendous amount of guilt. (One of the reasons organizations hire outplacement counselors is to deal with that guilt.)

Much of this obsolescence and guilt can be avoided if we teach employees to take back control of their careers and never again give control to the organization. There is tremendous wasted potential in the stagnated mature professional. If you turn just one of these individuals around and get them to move in a positive direction, you can save the organization a great deal of money and the individual a loss of self-esteem. If the stagnated person is a manager, think about the people who report to them and the poor leadership they have received. What are the results on morale and productivity of those employees who have less than positive supervision?

What Career Development Can Do for the Young, Skilled Worker

In an engineering organization these are the young, entry-level technicians who say, "I think I want to become an engineer and I'm not sure whether or not I have the skills to be an engineer. If I do, where and how do I get the training?" In the city government, such an employee may be a junior analyst and have to decide whether to move up to be a principal analyst. Often fairly traditional academic or educational coaching is the key to helping them decide what direction take.

Many young skilled and semiskilled workers are adrift when it comes to career planning. Managers and supervisors are often so focused on the day-to-day demands of the organization that they have little time to offer guidance and counseling. Participation in a career planning program can help workers to understand the needs and opportunities of the organization and to learn how to find and utilize local educational resources that will enable them to gain needed skills.

Career Development Is Even for the Specialized Knowledge Worker

Specialized knowledge workers have become highly visible in the world of work. Computer scientists, for example, are even starting to come in pairs! They may be a husband and wife who have advanced degrees in computer science, his and her BMWs, a townhouse right in the area, and a nice summer place an hour's drive away. They may not have children, but they are thinking about starting a family and what a family is going to do to their combined income of over $120,000 a year.

These are people who have been the prey of the headhunter and they are now asking, "Should I go with the next recruiter who calls? Am I becoming too overspecialized in my job? Now that I have all of these material things, is there something else for me that is more important than money?"

Many of these young computer specialists have made three job moves in the last three years, and they may work within a half mile of where they used to work. They can stay in the same townhouse and get a $5,000 annual raise with each move. But they are not in control of their careers—the recruiter is in control. They are very specialized in their profession, and this specialization is a major reason they get recruited from one place to another. Unfortunately, they could become overspecialized.

Today, the half-life of software is about six months. If a technology professional becomes too focused on a program that is company- or department-specific, he or she is in real danger of being left behind as technology continues to change at a rapid pace. The good news is that a career planning and development program has the very real potential of assisting the young computer professional to take control of and manage their career so they will not become obsolete.

Step 2

Assess the Organization's Need for Career Development

In Step 1, we examined the differing perspectives of career development that are associated with the individual's position in the organization. We also identified typical individuals who can benefit from career development activities. Now let us turn to formally assessing the need for career development in the organization. In my experience, it is the perceived need for career development that is most important.

In a typical organization, the first steps toward career development are often a discussion between the CEO and the human resources executive. The CEO says, "I have been getting some feedback that some of our employees don't know how to develop their careers here. Can your group put together a career development program?" The HR executive then goes to the employment manager and the training manager and asks, "Can you put a career development program together for us?" Both managers are good team players and agree to help. The employment manager has read Bolles' *What Color Is Your Parachute?* and Keirsey and Bates' *Please Understand Me,* so he suggests that each employee read the two books and then "develop their careers." The training manager suggests that the company adapt its very good Project Management course and change its name to "Career Management." The problem is that each of these managers has looked to their own, somewhat narrow, experience base for an answer.

Let me suggest a more systematic process, designed to acknowledge and accommodate the views and needs of employees at all levels in the organization.

Establishing a Career Development Task Force or Advisory Committee

In order to set the stage for a full-scale career development needs assessment, it is often useful to form an organizational task force or advisory committee. This is frequently a group of middle managers who have a strong stake in and strong opinions about any career development program that the organization might want to establish. In forming the task force, individuals who are invited to join the group should be selected on the basis of the guidelines shown in table 3.

Twelve to fifteen members is an optimal number for the career development task force, and it should include a few members from HR (e.g., the employment manager or the staff member responsible for the organization's job posting system, and the equal opportunity officer or the individual responsible for affirmative action programs).

Table 3   Guidelines for Choosing a Task Force

- Represent all major sectors of the organization, such as sales, finance, etc.
- Choose leaders whose opinions and ideas are respected by other employees in their department or division. These people may or may not be in formal positions of power.
- Draw from that group of managers who are friendly to the HR function, not those who tend to view the expenditure of funds on "overhead" or "discretionary" activities rather than the direct delivery of the organization's products or services as a waste of money.
- Select those who are willing to contribute the time and effort to attend all of the task force meetings and participate in the process.

When recruiting task force members, it is usually best not to ask department or division heads to nominate members from their areas. Having a task delegated to an assistant by a busy department manager might be an easy thing to do, but too often results in a member who just goes through the motions and is not really interested.

A better selection process would be to ask the senior organization development specialist who has knowledge of opinion leaders to use his or her powers of persuasion to attract the appropriate persons to the task force. If there is no organization development function in the organization, this task might fall to the vice president or director of human resources. It is important that the person in this role

- Knows who the opinion leaders are in each division or department
- Has ready access to and respect from the organization's president or CEO

The senior organization development specialist (or someone in a comparable role) should chair the task force during its meetings. The career development project leader, whether a consultant or internal staff member, should serve as an advisor, offering staff support to the task force.

We will revisit the task force after moving to the executive level in our quest to assess the need for career development.

Assessing the Career Development Views of Top Management

It is imperative that the initial view of career development to be examined be that of the organization's policy-making group—the top five to seven executives. These often include the chief executive officer and the vice presidents of finance, operations, sales, marketing, engineering or research and development, and human resources. The career development project leader usually asks the senior organization development specialist to set up a private one-hour meeting with each of the top executives of the organization. In some cases, the senior organization development specialist can sit in on the meetings; in other cases, especially if the career development project leader is an outside consultant, the executives may be more candid in their conversations if the session is strictly one-on-one.

As we saw in the preceding chapter, there may be as many definitions of career development as there are people. For this reason, it is often useful to begin the top-management career development needs assessment with some education. Some suggested topics for the interview are shown in table 4.

After conducting these top management interviews, the career development project leader analyzes the responses and prepares a summary of the top management views for presentation to task force members.

Assessing the Career Development Needs of Middle Management

It is during the first meeting of the career development task force (usually a three-hour or half-day session) that we find the best

Table 4   Guidelines for Interviewing Top Management

General Topics for Discussion

- Background of the interviewer and the project
- Summary of the five views of career development
- Concept of empowering employees to take charge of their own careers
- General description of a popular and effective career development process

Specific Issues to Be Determined

- The executive's personal views on career development
- Specific problems or issues that career development should address
- Specific groups or classifications of employees that should be targeted
- Specific tools or techniques (testing, manuals, etc.) that should be employed
- Specific tools or techniques that should be avoided
- Whether to use outside consultants
- Whether to use local college or university staff
- Whether to hire career development professionals as employees
- Whether to train the organization's human resource generalists to deliver career development
- Whether to train supervisors and managers to deliver career development

Final Questions to Be Answered

- When I am reporting the views of top management to our career development task force, may I quote you?
- Are there any other points or suggestions that you would like me to pass along to the career development task force?

opportunity to conduct the middle management career development needs assessment. The senior organization development specialist usually chairs this meeting with the career development project leader providing the content advice. An outline of the first task force meeting is presented in table 5.

The task force meeting will then shift to a group needs assessment interview, as shown in table 6.

Table 5   Guidelines for the Middle Management Task Force Meeting

- Introduce task force members.
- Introduce career development project leader.
- Outline meeting agenda.
- Provide background and reasons for the project.
- Summarize the five views of career development.
- Describe a popular and effective career development process.

**Table 6   Guidelines for the Middle Management
Needs Assessment Interview**

- How do individuals in the task force view career development?
- What specific problems or issues should career development address?
- What specific groups or classifications of employees need career development most?
- Are there specific tools or techniques that we should use for career development?
- Are there specific tools or techniques that we should avoid?
- How should the program be staffed?
- What role should supervisors and managers play in employee career development?

At this point in the meeting, the project leader, who has been capturing the middle manager's views on a flip chart, now presents the results of the top management needs assessment, pointing out the similarities and differences between the middle and top managers. The differences in these views, if significant, are discussed, and the career development project leader indicates the importance of next assessing the career development needs of the organization's rank-and-file employees. The task force members are asked to suggest any additional topics and questions that they think ought to be added to this third level of needs assessment.

A follow-up meeting should be scheduled for one month later to review the results of the employee needs assessment and present a suggested career development program for the task force's review and consideration.

Assessing the Career Development Needs of Employees

In order to get a clear picture of the expressed needs of employees in general for career development services, it is important to poll a representative sample of the organization's employee population. One method that works well, although it is not technically scientific, is to identify employees by major occupational clusters; work settings; gender, age, and ethnic background groups; and length of service with the organization. For example, if a significant group of employees are engineers, it would be important to include them in the sample. If the age range for engineers in the organization is from twenty-three to sixty-four years old, it would be important to examine the age brackets in which engineers cluster. Say, for example, the distribution of engineers by age group was as follows:

Age Bracket	Number of Engineers
21–25	2
26–30	26
31–35	5
36–40	37
41–45	31
46–50	7
51–55	34
56–60	3
61–65	1

To obtain a representative sample, you would want to make sure to include engineers in the age ranges of 26–30, 36–46, and 51–55. A similar process could be used to select other variables.

Table 7   Guidelines for Interviewing Employees

- What are the goals of career development?
- Who are the target groups?
- What are the career development issues of this organization?
- What is career development's relationship with other programs?
- What does the structure and content of career development look like?

In addition to the typical employees representative of the various categories within the organization, it would be a good idea to include occupational opinion leaders in the pool. They could be nominated by the task force as being typical of the potential users of the career development services.

Once a representative sample has been identified, the employees should be contacted by the designated interviewer or by a staff member of the human resources department to explain the reason for the interview. A one-hour interview should be scheduled for each sample member during the next two weeks, and a questionnaire could be sent to each individual ahead of time to be completed and brought along to the interview. The interview should be scheduled on company time, and, if necessary, the department head should be notified. One or two trained interviewers, preferably not employees of the organization, conduct the interviews. Topics to be covered in the interview are shown in table 7.

During the needs assessment interviews, employees are not asked their personal opinion on the topics. They are asked what they believe are the opinions of their colleagues about the topics and issues. This nondirect approach is less threatening to the employees and allows them to project their own needs in their response. In addition to the structured questions, employees are asked for any suggestions or questions that they might have. The responses of the rank-and-file employees to the needs assessment interviews are analyzed and compared and contrasted with the expressed needs of top

Should career counseling be provided by the employee's immediate supervisor?

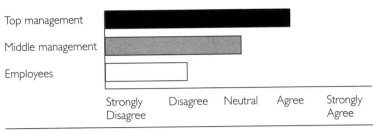

| | Strongly Disagree | Disagree | Neutral | Agree | Strongly Agree |

Top management
Middle management
Employees

Figure 10   Results of Three Levels of Needs Assessment

managers and the middle management task force. The results of the three levels of needs assessment can be presented on graphs or charts. The bar graph in figure 10 shows one example.

The Career Development Task Force—Phase 2

During the second meeting of the career development task force, the project leader presents the results of all three levels of the needs assessment and then introduces a model career development program with a structure and mix of elements that are consistent with the expressed needs of the three levels in the organization. The project leader then facilitates a discussion of the merits of the program and leads the group in considering potential modifications. Finally, when a consensus is reached, the implementation of a pilot career development program can begin.

Design a Program for the Organization

There is a range of methods for delivering career development to employees in organizations. Some methods are more appropriate for a particular organization than others. Here we will present an overview of several techniques.

Workshops

Workshops are, in my opinion, the most effective and efficient way of delivering career development to employees. Workshops require skilled trainers for delivery and involve experiential exercises and sharing of information among participants. Workshops are less expensive than individual one-on-one career counseling—the major cost is in time away from the job—and individuals learn much more in a workshop setting. Participants learn not only from the leader but from the other participants as well. They also learn by participating in a variety of group activities.

Sometimes managers in an organization may assign an unskilled group facilitator to lead a workshop: "Well, here's the information, pass it around, you all read it, and if you have any questions, I'll answer them." Training sessions like that don't work very well. Trainers should have skills in group dynamics and knowledge of career development.

Some managers are hesitant to sponsor a program involving experiential exercises: "We don't want any of that touchy-feely stuff." Workshops don't have to be touchy-feely. They can be straightforward and to the point, while incorporating experiential exercises. Since I was trained in group dynamics during the encounter group movement of the 1960s, I am very aware of some real fears that people have about groups. You have to have clear boundaries in experiential exercises so that people don't reveal too much of themselves and then feel threatened and embarrassed. A rule of thumb that I use in workshops is to tell people only to talk about things they are comfortable sharing with other people. I find that if you conduct a career development workshop series over a four- or five-week period of time, the group cohesiveness grows, people feel more comfortable sharing, and the group as a whole evolves into a real support group.

The most significant concern about workshops from a manager's point of view is the amount of time an employee is away from the job. Employee time away from the job amounts to at least half of the total cost of a workshop-based career development program. The other half is made up of trainers' time, facilities, and materials. In spite of the cost in participant time, I still feel that workshops are probably the most effective and efficient method of conducting career development programs.

In figure 11, I have presented guidelines for delivering a career development workshop model. This workshop design has evolved

Time Interval	Career Activity	Development Phase
Week 1	Half-day workshop	*Assessment* • Skills • Values • Interests • Work or management style
	Review data	
Week 2	Half-day workshop	*Exploration* • Identify five options • Field research • Reality testing
	Field research	
Week 3	Half-day workshop	*Focus* • Best match • Realistic goal • Reality testing
	Planning	
Week 4	One-hour individual counseling session	*Strategy* • What? • Why? • How? • When? • Who?
	Prepare Presentation	
Week 5	Half-day workshop	*Presentation* • Describe strategy plan • Demonstrate behavior • Receive feedback • Get appropriate support

Figure 11 Guidelines for Delivering a Career Development Workshop

over the years. We have found that a five-week interval is the ideal time frame for most people. Figure 11 shows a half-day workshop during the first three weeks and again during the fifth week. There is a one-hour individual coaching session in the fourth week. In addition to the formal workshops and individual coaching session, there are other activities such as reviewing data between the first and second weeks, doing field research between the second and third weeks, writing career strategy plans between the third and fourth weeks, and, finally, implementing a plan after the fifth week. Note that the workshop process is organized around a simple, five-step program: assessment, exploration, focus, strategy, and presentation.

During the 1970s, the time frame of the workshop was initially spread over an academic semester (seventeen weeks) or a quarter (ten or eleven weeks). There was a very high attrition rate of the participants who started a seventeen-week program. Since the time frame has gone down to five weeks, there is virtually no attrition. In the beginning of the workshop, it is important to communicate the assumption that all participants will finish the workshop.

About two weeks before the start of the workshop, there is usually a two-hour orientation session. During the orientation, the amount of commitment and homework required in the workshop is explained, and the participants are exposed to a typical small-group workshop activity. Those employees who are too busy or not motivated enough to complete the entire workshop series are encouraged to skip this workshop and enroll at a later date.

Career Counseling

Even if the major method an organization uses to deliver its career development program to employees is the workshop, the organization is usually going to have to provide some individual counseling or coaching. Individual counseling requires skilled counselors, is expensive, and involves confidentiality of information. You will note in figure 11, "Guidelines for Delivering a Career Development

Workshop," that there is one individual counseling session during week four. We have found that in just about every single group activity—whether it is a train-the-trainer workshop, a management development workshop, a career development workshop for employees, or a class at a university—there are always one or two people who say, "I need to see you at the break. I have a problem or situation that is unique, and I would like to talk to you individually." In group outplacement workshops, the same thing occurs. There are some individuals who just cannot deal effectively with certain things in a group setting. There are concerns that are either so unique, or the person feels they are so unique, that they must be addressed in private.

Career counselors usually hold a master's degree in counseling or psychology and have completed graduate courses in assessment and group process. Their skill base is much broader than just the career planning or job search areas. Counselors are trained to work with individuals involved in a wide variety of issues and transitions. Some career counselors are also therapists who can effectively deal with individuals who may have serious emotional problems. All career counselors are expected to be able to recognize problems that are beyond the scope of their expertise and refer clients to competent sources of help. Professional career counselors are trained to administer and interpret assessment instruments such as the *Myers-Briggs Type Indicator®* (MBTI®) and the *Strong Interest Inventory®*.

Career Coaches

The role and responsibilities of the career coach are more narrow in scope than those of the counselor. Career coaches do not necessarily have graduate training in counseling or psychology. Their job is to guide an individual through a short-term job transition or a long-term career transition. The focus of the coach is not on more pervasive life issues and life transitions. Like the counselor, the coach is trained to ask questions of the client and listen for the direction that the client wants to take. While both the counselor and coach are careful to avoid directing the client toward a particular goal, the coach has the responsibility of teaching the client specific planning, exploration, and job search techniques.

Adjunct Career Development Trainers

For the past eighteen to twenty years, we have been developing and employing what I call "adjunct trainers" to staff organizational career development programs. Like the career coach, the adjunct career development trainer uses career development and planning techniques. While I think organizations will continue to need some access to professionally trained counselors, in reality, this access may come more and more from consultants. Organizations with career development programs are no longer hiring significant numbers of counselors with master's or doctorate degrees to be on staff. Many lay employees have both an interest in career development and the skills and education to colead workshops. With minimal training, these adjunct trainers can learn career development principles and career coaching skills.

The Issue of Confidentiality

During the training of professional counselors, adjunct counselors, or career coaches, a significant amount of time should be devoted to discussing the area of confidentiality. I have found that the number of confidentiality issues that come up in organizational career development programs is not very great, but the issues are important when they do come up. Several years ago, I worked with a top-secret government organization. In the course of my role as a career counselor, I had two different contacts with employees who did things and said things in counseling sessions that led me to believe they were psychotic. In both instances, I took their security badges away from them so they could not reenter the facility. In both these cases, the individuals had told me something in confidence that caused me to believe they were dangerous. I may have been wrong in my assessment, but I chose to err in the direction of violating the individual's confidentiality rather than risking the safety of a significant number of people. Although this example may be extreme, career counselors, coaches, and adjunct trainers may have to deal with some confidentiality issues and may have to decide when it is appropriate to intervene.

Two or three other times when confidentiality came up in my personal experience in an organizational career development program, it involved theft. If you as a career counselor, coach, or adjunct trainer are an employee of an organization and someone comes to you and tells you he or she has stolen property, you are bound as an employee of the organization to report it. It is a generally accepted part of your employment agreement. If you suspect an employee is about to confess a crime to you, it is a good idea to say something like this:

> Could you wait just a minute and let me tell you something. You know, even though our relationship is confidential, if you tell me that you've committed some crime like theft, I'm required to report it to the appropriate officials of the organization, and you need to know that.

I have been in this situation more than once, and each time I've given this speech, the employee has responded similarly to this: "Yes, I understand that. But I'm feeling so bad—or the guilt is so bad—I need to tell someone. I want to tell you about it, and I know you need to report it."

Some professional counselors believe that all managers want to pry information from them that they can use against employees. In reality, a very small percentage of managers in organizations will do this, and coaches need to be prepared to say no. I have organized and supervised groups of counselors and chaired counselor meetings in organizations. In almost every single meeting, we discussed confidentiality. When leading workshops, I always tell employees that I will not repeat anything that they say in the workshop, and I hope that they will not repeat anything that other participants say. In the counseling situation, I try to keep everything confidential unless a crime has been committed or others are endangered. Most of the time career counselors, coaches, and trainers won't have any problem with confidentiality.

Management Discussions

Since the late 1970s, the idea of a manager's involvement in the career development of employees has been growing in acceptance. Initial efforts in this area centered around assigning the manager the responsibility of meeting with an employee to have a career discussion. For a management discussion to be effective, it is necessary to have trained managers who are objective, have a broad view of the employee's options, and are motivated.

The manager is in the ideal position to assess the employees to give them feedback. Managers spend all their time with their employees; HR specialists do not. The problem is that managers need to be trained to lead career discussions.

One of the most important things to teach a manager is to be objective. Managers sometimes feel they are being paid to have all the answers, so they view having all the answers as appropriate behavior. Managers are also focused on upward mobility—gaining more power and authority in their jobs—and they tend to hold the opinion that all employees have these aspirations.

In order for managers to lead productive career development discussions, they have to learn to be objective and to accept the individual uniqueness in people. A significant area that hampers managers as career discussion leaders is their lack of a broad view of employee options. Many managers believe that the employee's only appropriate option is moving up to the next level—the supervisor becomes the manager, the manager becomes the director, the director becomes the vice president, and so on. They have a hard time seeing that the employee could go to work for somebody else in another department, go to work in another company, or even change career fields. In order for managers to successfully lead career discussions and conduct career coaching, we have to help them take the blinders off. They must understand the wide range of options that employees have. The most effective way of training managers is to put them through a career assessment, planning, and development process themselves. If the manager has used the career development process on his or her own career, then it is much easier and more natural to use the process with an employee.

Manager as Career Coach

Major aspects of career development programs in organizations during the next decade are going to involve the manager as a career coach. Career coaching will not be the same as the informal career discussions of the 1970s and 1980s. The manager as career coach has a role analogous to that of the football coach—that of motivator and strategist. The manager can't "play the game" for the employee but needs to be on the sidelines to offer advice, counsel, and encouragement. Table 8 outlines six manager coaching roles.

How do you motivate managers to be effective career coaches? What is in it for those managers? My belief is that you must hold the manager accountable for doing career coaching and leading career discussions. The key, I believe, is the manager's performance appraisal. Not only should you measure the managers on how good they are at cost containment, completing new assignments, and affirmative

Table 8 The Six Coaching Roles of the Manager

Role	Task
Assessor	Identifies employee's skills and gives accurate feedback
Information provider	Informs employee about options and barriers
Referral agent	Refers employee to outside source of information
Guide	Encourages employee to focus on appropriate and available goal
Teacher	Tutors employee in designing and implementing a plan
Developer	Assigns employee to developmental tasks

action, you should have a section in the performance appraisal form specifically focused on the manager's performance in developing subordinates. Managers have to know what they personally have to gain by developing their employees. They have to be rewarded for developing employees (and maybe punished if they don't).

Workbooks

In every organization that decides to implement a career development program, almost without exception, a self-paced workbook for employees to use in their individual career development is created. Unfortunately, most of these workbooks end up gathering dust on the shelf. Self-paced workbooks require a tremendous amount of self-discipline and sticking to priorities, and my experience is that they generally don't work. The reason that they don't work is not because of any problem with the content—the problem is with the concept. People tend to need individual contact in learning, either in a classroom or one-on-one. Sometimes we need workbooks that go along with the individual career coaching or workshops, and I think that workbooks are important and effective when used in *support of other activities*.

Career Path Systems

A career path is typically a road map for an employee to use to move up within the organization. Career pathing assumes that up is the only way; very few career pathing programs show flexible paths that move either laterally or downward. A career pathing program assumes that an employee stays within the organization. It is appropriate only in a closed system, like the military or a government agency.

All that is required for career development in this type of system is that the employee have enough information about the career paths. I have talked with many organizations that had not started their career development programs because they didn't have their career paths described yet, or their job descriptions weren't ready yet. Career pathing systems also provide one of the biggest excuses employees use for not doing career planning: "If we are not given the information, how can we develop a plan?" There are too many employees coming to career planning workshops expecting to sit down and have the instructor pass out all the career paths to them, and then all they have to do is figure out how to get from here to there. It is better to teach employees to figure out all the various formal and informal paths and opportunities both from within and from outside the organization. Effective career planning programs teach employees how to research and discover information that they will need to plan and develop their own careers.

Educational Programs

Career development is a process that helps people figure out where they want to go and how they want to get there. Sometimes the way you want to get there is through an educational program. Most large organizations have either in-house educational programs or a referral system to outside programs. Some of the outside educational resources that can assist an employee in attaining a career goal include community colleges, universities, adult education programs, and professional societies. If I worked at a community college and you came to me for career counseling, it would be very easy for me to see you in terms of which of my college courses you should enroll in. If I worked at a private school that taught computer programming and you came in for some career counseling, I'd be thinking, I wonder what kind of computer programmer this person ought to be. Educational programs are not an end in themselves. They are often the means to an end. Employees must learn first to develop a clear vision of an attainable goal, and then how to choose the appropriate educational program to attain the goal.

Computerized Career Information Systems

The most well-known computerized career information systems are SIGI, from Educational Testing Service in Princeton, New Jersey; DISCOVER for Organizations from American College Testing in Iowa City, Iowa; various state Computer Information Systems; and Career Point from Conceptual Systems in Maryland. These systems are widely available and are no longer very expensive. I've found that they are good adjuncts to career development programs. Most systems contain files of curricula and courses that lead to specific occupations. However, I have found that their major value in an organization is for employees who want to help their children with career decisions. It does get those parents into your career center to introduce them to a rather safe way to initiate a contact about their own careers, and this is valuable in itself.

Promote the Program Internally

As we saw in Step 1, there is not clear agreement on the definition of career development. In Step 2, we saw that there can be even less agreement on the need for career development in the organization. In Step 3, we reviewed a variety of techniques that can be used to deliver career development. In Step 4, we will discuss some creative ideas about promoting career development within the organization.

Pilot Program

Installing career development in the organization as a pilot program has a number of advantages. First, many organizations are hesitant to publicize any program or activity they may subsequently have to abolish and thus deal with the resulting negative impact on employee motivation. Second, a pilot program can easily be delivered by consultants or contractors, avoiding the necessity of assigning new duties to otherwise fully occupied staff or hiring new staff. Third, the temporary nature of a pilot program will allow and encourage the modification and fine-tuning of the program to fit the unique needs of the organization's employees, or allow for the accommodation of the training delivery mechanisms currently in place in the organization. In short, the organization can quickly mount a pilot career development program without making a long-term and expensive commitment to a process, the ultimate effects of which may be unknown or unclear.

The Role of the Task Force in a Pilot Career Development Program

In Step 2, we introduced the concept of the career development task force as a vehicle for assessing the need for organizational career development. This same task force can be an important con-tributor to the success of a pilot career development program. The middle managers and opinion leaders on the task force can con-tribute to the structure of the pilot program through their knowl-edge of not only what is *needed* by the organization but also what is *possible* in the organization.

It is important that the content and structure of the pilot work-shop substantially parallel the configuration of the ultimate work-shop that will be available to the employees. A description of a model workshop was presented in Step 3. While the "ideal" career development workshop is spread out over a five-week period, it is possible to compress the pilot workshop into a two-day time frame. While this compressed version will allow the task force members to experience and evaluate all of the assessment instru-ments, experiential exercises, and planning activities, it will not allow time for extensive homework, field research, or planning.

If the program is conducted properly, the participants should develop an appreciation for the process. If the task force members like the program, they will promote it by word of mouth in their respective departments and divisions. They in effect will take "ownership" of the career development program, and it will become their program, and not a program instituted or mandated by HR.

Information Sessions

Once the task force has evaluated and, if appropriate, modified the career development program, the program can be announced to the organization. Some common methods of announcing the program are by memo, newsletter, or electronic mail. But the most effective method of announcing the program is to conduct one- to two-hour information sessions in each of the major departments or divisions. Often, they can be included in regularly scheduled staff meetings.

An ideal information session would be hosted by the department "opinion leader" for a particular department, who is also a member of the task force. The task force member could introduce the project leader or a workshop leader, who will deliver a short presentation describing the program and field questions and comments by the employees and managers in attendance. The presenter should be direct about commenting not only on what is included in the program but also on what is not included. Guidelines for announcing the career development program to the organization can be found in table 9.

Brown Bag Luncheon Presentations

The brown bag luncheon presentation is a lower-key method of promoting the career development program to employees in the organization. The sessions are held during the lunch hour in a room near the cafeteria or other location where food can be obtained. Instead of starting with a formal presentation about the

Table 9   Guidelines for the Information Session

- Discuss the purpose of the Career Development process.
- Describe the process, using a flow chart if necessary.
- Bring up some typical employee issues that career development addresses.
- Discuss the amount of commitment and homework required.
- Present sample career strategy plans.
- Ask for questions and comments.
- Explain how to enroll in the program.

career development process, a hands-on demonstration of one of the instruments or exercises from the program is given. For example, the presentation might include taking and interpreting a short personality or management style instrument, or viewing and discussing a goal-setting film. The point is that the activity or instrument should be useful by itself, in addition to being a significant aspect of the career development program. The brown bag luncheon presentation should conclude with a short description of the career development program and brief comments on how interested employees can sign up to attend a workshop or obtain individual career development assistance.

Acknowledge the Individual Employee's Emotions

Employee career development is simple, but not easy. Table 10 shows the stages of career development in two situations: first, when career planning is welcome and voluntary; and second, when career development or a career transition is not voluntary, as when a company downsizes or an employee suffers a disabling injury.

Employees experience predictable emotional reactions to downsizing, layoff, or any other involuntary career transition. There are three significant traumas that most normal individuals will experience, either directly or indirectly, in their lives. These traumas are outlined in table 11.

Table 10 The Sequence of Career Development

Voluntary Career Transition	Involuntary Career Transition
• Assessment of skills	• Ventilation of feelings
• Exploration of options	• Assessment of skills
• Focus on appropriate goal	• Exploration of options
• Strategy implementation	• Focus on appropriate goal
	• Strategy implementation

Table 11 Traumatic Events That Affect Most Normal Individuals

- Death of a close relative
- Divorce or termination of a long-term relationship
- Termination or layoff from a job or career

Anyone who has read the work of Elizabeth Kubler-Ross, including her most famous, *On Death and Dying*, will recognize that our responses to all three of these traumas are often surprisingly similar. These reactions to trauma are outlined in table 12.

Our society has many rituals such as wakes and funerals that allow us to deal with our feelings about death and dying. We are even starting to have some rituals such as final divorce celebrations that help us cope with the emotions associated with marital dissolution. But we have yet to develop rituals for dealing with job loss. For this reason, a good career development model should include, where appropriate, a vehicle for surfacing and dealing with the emotions associated with job loss.

Whenever an employee is involved in career planning, career development, or career transition as a result of events that the employee perceives to be out of his or her control, it is important to consider the emotions that may be present. If a group of employees are doing career planning because their department or specialty is being abolished, it is appropriate to start the career workshop

Table 12 Typical Responses to Major Life Traumas

- Shock
- Immobilization
- Disbelief
- Denial
- Bargaining
- Anger
- Frustration
- Grieving

---

with an activity designed to surface emotions. One useful technique is to have the workshop leader poll each participant on the specific feelings that each experienced when they were first notified that their job was being eliminated. The workshop leader records each feeling on a flip chart and tapes the pages to the walls of the training room. Many of the feelings will be negative, such as anger, shock, disbelief, and sadness. Others may be more positive, such as relief.

This group process allows many of the participants to listen to the feelings of others and discover what they were experiencing themselves but may have been hesitant to acknowledge or talk about. Most significantly, the participants find out that normal employees, when confronted with an unexpected or controllable career transition, usually experience many of the feelings and emotions that many think are only associated with divorce or death. They learn that these feelings are normal and predictible and need to be surfaced and dealt with before an individual can move ahead with formal career planning.

Guide Employee's Assessment Process

Although employees often would like to start their personal career development efforts at the implementation stage, it is critical that they start at the beginning of the assessment stage. For the developer of a pilot career development program, this is the sixth step, which involves assessing the characteristics and strengths of the individual. One self-assessment tool that is recommended is to have employees complete an Employee Career Profile, a sample of which is shown in figure 12. Appendix A provides a master Employee Career Profile for duplication.

Career satisfaction and success depends on how compatible the career is with the individual's career values, occupational interests, skills, and work or management style.

Career Values Assessment

The importance of career values in job satisfaction can't be over-remphasized. A few years ago I worked with an attorney who was

Section I.　CAREER ASSESSMENT

1. List your six to eight most important career values:

   Creativity, Challenging problems, Make decisions, Exercise competence,
   Work with others, Influence people

2. List your six to eight strongest career interests:

   Realtor, Insurance agent, Sales manager, Public administrator,
   Juvenile parole officer

3. List your six to eight most highly motivated skills:

   Plan, organize; Teach, train; Observe; Interview; Mediate; Classify

4. List your highest one or two work or management styles:　Creative

Section II.　CAREER EXPLORATION

1. List at least five jobs or careers that you can pursue:

   Realtor, Insurance agent, Sales manager, Teacher, Trainer,
   Human resources administrator

Section III.　CAREER FOCUS—YOUR GOAL

1. List the option from section II that fits you the best: What is your goal?

   Realtor

2. Why is this the best goal for you? List evidence (skills, values, etc.) that
   show the above goal is the very best possible goal for you:　Work with others;
   influence people's values; plan and organize; be creative

Section IV.　CAREER STRATEGY AND IMPLEMENTATION PLAN

1. How will you get to your goal? What specific behavior will you engage
   in to attain your goal? Be clear and specific about what you will do.

   I will take Principles of Real Estate at city college.

2. When will each step to your career goal occur?

   Classes will begin September 14.

3. Who will be affected by your plan? Who can help you in your plan?

   I will talk to Mr. Johnson, my business administration instructor, who also has a
   real estate license. I will talk to my spouse about this night class.

Figure 12　Sample Employee Career Profile

considering leaving the practice of law. This was a very successful attorney (at least in terms of income) who was coincidentally about age 40 and going through a divorce. He specialized in representing corporations that were being sued by individuals. This attorney came to me with the assumption that what he needed from me was a list of new jobs he might move to. I thought it would be useful to first assess some of his career values and administered the Career Values Card Sort and Motivated Skills Card Sort assessment instruments (which can be found in appendices E and F). The results revealed that his two highest values were "Moral fulfillment" and "Help others"—not a very good fit for the type of corporate law he was practicing. On the other hand, his motivated skills—analyzing, writing, persuading, and selling—actually fit his current job quite well.

Consequently, he looked at the possibility of continuing the practice of law but changing his specialty or the firm he would work for. He was even willing to take a substantial cut in pay in order to work in a job that fit his values. He ended up practicing the same type of law, but now for a law firm that represented plaintiffs in product liability cases, that is, representing the people who had been harmed, not the corporation that was accused of being at fault.

A Simple Method of Prioritizing Career Values

Table 13 provides a list of career values used by career development experts to help employees assess and prioritize their own particular career values. These career values are also used in the Career Values Card Sort, which is found in appendix E. These perforated cards can be separated into a set of 42 values cards. The same cards can then be quickly sorted by the employee into the five categories presented on the category cards, as shown in the example layout in figure 13. While there are a variety of ways that the employee can organize and analyze career values, sorting the cards into the five categories is a quick and painless way to identify and isolate the

Table 13 Career Values

Independence	Make decisions
Exercise competence	Work alone
Creative expression	Affiliation
Challenging problems	Power and authority
Job tranquility	Community
Precision work	Competition
Work under pressure	Location
Intellectual status	Stability
Physical challenge	Profit, gain
Change and variety	Help society
Status	Time, freedom
Knowledge	General creativity
Security	Artistic creativity
Fast pace	Supervision
Advancement	Adventure
Friendships	Recognition
Aesthetics	Moral fulfillment
Public contact	Work with others
Excitement	Higher earnings anticipated
Influence people	Help others
Work on frontiers of knowledge	

individual's highest or most important six or seven career values. The career values determined from table 13 or the card sort in appendix E can be entered in item 1 of section I in the Employee Career Profile.

The significance of career values to career planning will be made very clear when we reach the goal setting and planning segment of the career development model. For now, here are a few general points to remember:

■ Most of our career values are learned early in life and some of them change as we grow older and face new issues and decisions.

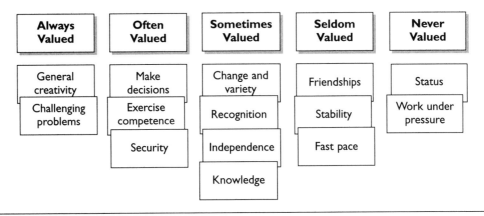

Always Valued	Often Valued	Sometimes Valued	Seldom Valued	Never Valued
General creativity	Make decisions	Change and variety	Friendships	Status
Challenging problems	Exercise competence	Recognition	Stability	Work under pressure
	Security	Independence	Fast pace	
		Knowledge		

Figure 13   Sample Career Values Card Sort Layout

■ Using the simple card sort allows individuals to quickly prioritize the career values they hold at this point in time.

■ Most forty-year-olds are engaged in occupations that were chosen when they were twenty.

Career Interest Assessment

While career values represent strong principles that can be associated with many occupations and jobs, career interests are often apparent in the basic tasks or environments that attract us to some occupations and repel us from others. Many practitioners see individual career interests as being more stable than career values.

There are many excellent career or vocational interest inventories that are commercially available. Some of the most reliable and valid instruments, such as the *Strong Interest Inventory*, are only available to professional counselors. If the reader has access to one of these standardized instruments, the results can be entered in item 2 of section I on the Employee Career Profile. If a standardized career interest instrument is not available, the employee can review

	Definitely Interested	Probably Interested	Indifferent	Probably Not Interested	Definitely Not Interested
Realtor	☑	☐	☐	☐	☐
Physical education teacher	☐	☐	☐	☐	☑
Physicist	☐	☐	☐	☐	☑
Landscape gardener	☐	☐	☐	☑	☐
Airline ticket agent	☐	☐	☑	☐	☐
Juvenile parole officer	☐	☑	☐	☐	☐
Telephone operator	☐	☐	☑	☐	☐
Public administrator	☐	☑	☐	☐	☐
Bookkeeper	☐	☐	☐	☐	☑
Recreation leader	☐	☑	☐	☐	☐
Farmer	☐	☐	☐	☑	☐
Insurance agent	☑	☐	☐	☐	☐
Sales manager	☑	☐	☐	☐	☐
Pharmacist	☐	☐	☐	☑	☐

Figure 14   Sample Checklist of Career Interests

the Checklist of Career Interests shown in appendix B (which can be used as a master for duplication) and check the six to eight that hold the strongest attraction, as shown in the sample, figure 14. The employee can then enter the names of those careers in item 2. Employees and counselors should note, however, that the fact that an occupation or career is attractive to an individual doesn't mean it is the right or ideal job for him or her. What it does mean is that there may be a strong element or elements of that job that should also be in the job that the individual pursues. For instance, just

Table 14 Motivated Skills

Plant, cultivate	Entertain, perform	Use mechanical abilities
Plan, organize	Monitor	Treat, nurse
Produce skilled crafts	Read for information	Implement
Observe	Perceive intuitively	Supervise
Tend animals	Proofread, edit	Portray images
Maintain records	Host/hostess	Test
Count	Make decisions	Act as a liaison
Teach, train	Counsel	Visualize
Transport	Sell	Stage shows
Interview for information	Deal with feelings	Evaluate
Mediate	Negotiate	Use carpentry abilities
Classify	Expedite	Synthesize
Initiate change	Design	Generate ideas
Make arrangements	Compose music	Estimate
Prepare food	Motivate	Write
Budget	Analyze	Use physical coordination and agility

because I personally find being a broadcaster attractive, it doesn't mean I should seek a job as a radio announcer. Rather, it does mean that I like to talk and use words in my daily activities—as I do.

Motivated Skills Assessment

While all of us have spent some time examining how competent we are at using certain skills, most of us have never carefully considered a second dimension of skills—how motivated we are to use them. Since our skills are generally the primary reason that an employer hires us, it is important to analyze them.

Appendix F, the Motivated Skills Card Sort, contains a master set of over fifty generic transferable motivated skills cards and eight category cards. The individual skills are listed in table 14. These perforated cards can be separated into a set of skills cards and quickly sorted by the employee.

Although the process used in the Motivated Skills Card Sort is more complex than the one used in the Career Values Card Sort, it can yield a very accurate personal picture of motivated skills. In using this instrument, it is important to follow the sorting activities exactly in the following sequence:

1. Place the five motivation category cards in a vertical column on the left-hand side of a flat surface as illustrated in figure 15.

2. Sort the entire deck of motivated skills cards into five stacks immediately to the right of the five motivation category cards as illustrated in figure 16. Use the following criteria when sorting the cards into the five stacks:

   • Consider only how much you like to use the skill, or would like to use it if you could. Do *not* consider your competence at the skill.

   • Do *not* think about your current job or a job that you are considering when you engage in this exercise.

   • Strive to distribute the cards fairly evenly, ensuring that you have *at least* six cards in each of the five stacks.

3. Now place the three competency cards across the top of your work space as illustrated in figure 17.

4. In the next three activities, it is important to change the way you view these skills from how much you like to use them to how competent you are at using them. As illustrated in figure 18, take the top stack of skill cards and restack it into three piles according to how competent you are at using the skill. It is important to place at least two cards into each new stack.

5. Move down to the second stack of cards, to the right of the Enjoy Using Very Much category card. As in the previous activity, distribute this stack into three additional stacks, according to how competent you are at using the skill. Again, make sure that you place *at least* two cards in each stack, as shown in figure 19.

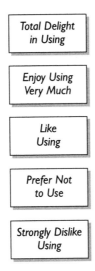

Figure 15   Motivated Skills Card Sort—Card Layout A

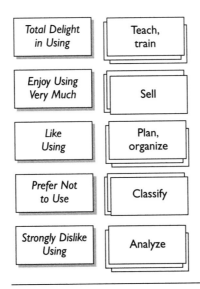

Figure 16   Motivated Skills Card Sort—Card Layout B

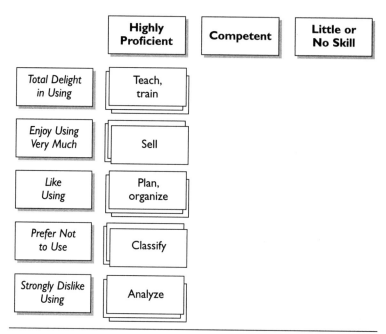

Figure 17　Motivated Skills Card Sort—Card Layout C

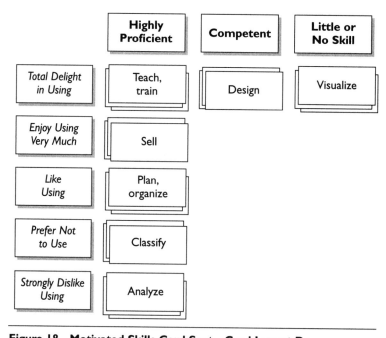

Figure 18　Motivated Skills Card Sort—Card Layout D

Building a Career Development Program

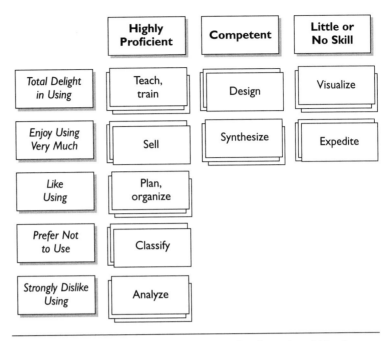

Figure 19 Motivated Skills Card Sort—The Completed Matrix

6. Move to the third, fourth, and fifth stacks and sort them to the right according to your competency, as you have done in steps 4 and 5. Again, be sure to include *at least* two skill cards in each stack. Your cards should now be distributed into a matrix similar to that shown in figure 20.

Now, write down six to eight of the skills from the upper left-hand corner of the completed matrix and enter them in item 3 of Section I of the Employee Career Profile in appendix A. Again, the significance of these motivated skills will be described in detail when we move to Step 8, the goal setting and planning segment. Until then, you should keep the following points in mind:

■ The motivated skills in the upper left-hand corner of the matrix are skills that you strive to use both on and off the job.

■ The more you can use these motivated skills at work, the happier you will be with your job assignment.

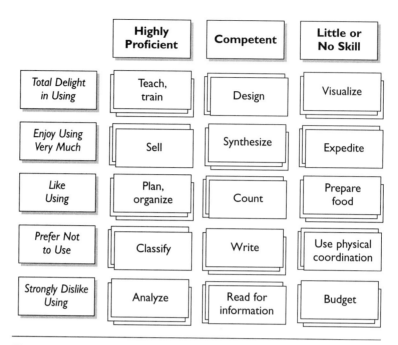

	Highly Proficient	Competent	Little or No Skill
Total Delight in Using	Teach, train	Design	Visualize
Enjoy Using Very Much	Sell	Synthesize	Expedite
Like Using	Plan, organize	Count	Prepare food
Prefer Not to Use	Classify	Write	Use physical coordination
Strongly Dislike Using	Analyze	Read for information	Budget

Figure 20   Motivated Skills Card Sort—The Completed Matrix

■ If you can't use your motivated skills on the job, you will use them at home or in volunteer activities.

■ The "burnout skills" in the lower-left-hand corner of the matrix are skills that you are good at but hate to use either on or off the job.

■ The more you have to use your burnout skills at work, the closer you come to quitting your job.

■ Your manager may not always be able to distinguish between your motivated skills and your burnout skills and may reward the use of burnout skills by giving you assignments to use them more.

■ The skills in the upper-right-hand corner (total delight in using, but little or no skill) should be developed and practiced.

■ The skills in the lower-right-hand corner (strongly dislike using and little or no skill) should be avoided.

Assessing Work Style or Management Style

The final element in our career assessment process—work style or management style—has also been called personality style or learning style. Whatever we call it, this personal style is the unique way that each individual prefers to interact with people and tasks.

While most managers say they hire people because of their skills, in actuality, much of the hiring decision rests on how well the job candidate's style fits the work environment. "We just clicked" is a rationale for hiring based on personal work style.

As with career interest assessment inventories, there are many excellent style assessment instruments. Some, like the well-researched *Myers-Briggs Type Indicator* (MBTI) are only available to professional counselors or individuals with specific training. If the reader has access to a style assessment instrument, the results can be entered into item 4 of section I of the Employee Career Profile.

For those who do not have access to a standardized style assessment instrument, appendix C contains a simple style assessment instrument, the Work Style Survey. A sample of a completed survey is shown in figure 21. This instrument allows the individual to assess his or her style according to the model of personality or work style in figure 22.

As with the other three assessment instruments, the significance of the Work Style Survey's results in the career planning process will be addressed directly in Step 8. Until then, the following general points should be kept in mind:

■ The work style score should *not* be used to select an occupation: For example, everyone with an Analytical style does not need to become an accountant—rather, the work style score should be an indicator of *what kind of* an accountant a person would be if that is the career he or she chose.

Directions

In each of the twelve questions on the next page, there are four descriptive words or terms. For each item, you are asked to choose the word that most people who know you would say accurately described you. Give that word 4 points and write the number next to the word. On the same question, choose the word or term that is the next best in describing you and give that word 3 points. Give the word that is next best at describing you 2 points. Finally, give the word that is least accurate in describing you 1 point. Follow the same process for all twelve questions.

Example

1. Logical **3**   Emotional **2**   Practical **1**   Intellectual **4**

Work Style Survey

	A		B		C		D	
1. Logical	3	Emotional	2	Practical	1	Intellectual	4
2. Systematic	1	Stimulating	3	Realistic	2	Creative	4
3. Careful	1	Responsive	2	Quick	3	Ingenious	4
4. Planful	1	Empathetic	3	Immediate	2	Future thinker	4
5. Calm	1	Feeling	2	Pragmatic	3	Big picture	4
6. Precise	1	Sociable	3	Here and now	2	Unique	4
7. Fact oriented	2	People person	1	Doer	3	Conceptualizer	4
8. Uses data	3	Uses charm	2	Gets results	1	Generate ideas	4
9. Good analyzer	3	Good listener	2	Type A	1	Original thinker	4
10. Info person	3	Warm	1	Energetic	2	Global thinker	4
11. Organized	1	Approachable	2	Resourceful	3	Bright	4
12. Competent	2	Nonthreatening	3	Hands-on	1	Innovator	4

Row A	**Analytical**—detailed and logical	Points	22
Row B	**Emotional**—sensitive and friendly	Points	26
Row C	**Action**—multitasked and quick	Points	24
Row D	**Creative**—big-picture and future-oriented	Points	48

Figure 21   Sample Work Style Survey

Analytical	Action
Detailed and logical	Multitasked and quick
Creative	**Emotional**
Big-picture and future-oriented	Sensitive and friendly

Figure 22   A Simple Model of Work Style

- A high score on a particular work style indicates a preference for a *style*, not a *skill level*: For example, someone with an Action work style could have excellent analytical skills, but would not necessarily have a preference for being analytical.
- The best teams generally include individuals with a variety of work styles.
- You can perform very well in a task or job that is opposite from your work style for a short period of time.
- Personality and work style are generally well-embedded characteristics that seldom change radically over a lifetime.
- It is possible for individuals to work toward balancing their work styles by developing the weaker elements.

Facilitate Employee's Exploration Process

A major strength of many of us in this society is the tendency to accept each task and challenge as it is presented to us and jump right in to solve the problem or do the job. While this may work well in many situations, it is not the best policy when the time comes to explore career options. We can look at exploring options as being analogous to eating at a buffet or salad bar. When we start down the buffet line, most of us have filled our plates before we get halfway through the line. But the most effective way to eat at a buffet would be to first walk down the line *without a plate*—to look at each dish, examine our appetites, consider any dietary restrictions, ask the cook about the contents of any exotic dish, and make up our minds on just which dishes we want—and then take a plate and start filling it with food.

Like the person in the buffet line, the career planner should explore all of the available options before making a decision. The exploration phase has two main parts: specifying a range of career options, and exploring the specifics of each career option.

Specifying the Range of Career Options

When we view our career or job options, most of us are wearing the proverbial blinders. Since we are socialized to be task oriented, it is much easier to focus on the current job or task than to develop an awareness of other options on the horizon or in our periphery. Some find it difficult to consider a job outside the company or industry; others find it difficult to consider moving to a different career. It is important to consider a wide range of options, even if we do not wish to make a radical career change, because it is important to ensure that the career or job that we ultimately focus on is arrived at through the process of choice. There are at least three methods that we as career professionals should advise our client of for specifying the range of options.

First, clients can take the assessment instruments that were discussed in Step 6 and examine the results. Some questions the results can help answer are: What jobs or careers are suggested by my career values? Are there some attractive occupations that came out of the Checklist of Career Interests? What jobs might demand some of my motivated skills? Which jobs would be most compatible with my style as indicated by the Work Style Survey? Which would be most compatible with my career values?

A second method involves counseling clients to talk to a number of friends and co-workers and asking them for suggestions on jobs and careers that might suit them. They can even elicit the opinions of people who do not know them well, if they first give them some details of their background. Table 15 contains some categories of individuals that they can enlist to assist them in two areas: exploring options and implementing a career change or job search plan.

A third method is to "just do it!" In employee career development workshops, I frequently give participants the assignment of coming up with five or six different career or job options. They are given very little direction regarding whether the careers or jobs chosen should be inside the company or outside, should involve

Table 15   Categories of People Who Could Be Starting Contacts for a Potential Network

• Relatives and in-laws	• Friends
• Former roommates	• Social acquaintances
• Neighbors	• Former neighbors
• Former classmates	• Alumni/alumnae
• Former teachers	• Former bosses
• Former co-workers	• Former employees
• Local business executives	• Your banker
• Your accountant	• Your lawyer
• Your rabbi or minister	• Your dentist
• Your insurance broker	• Fellow association members

skills the employee already has, or should be realistic. Participants are simply given a deadline to come up with the options—sometimes it is for next week's meeting; sometimes it is tomorrow; often it is right after lunch, today. I have found that the participants will almost always come up with the required options in the time specified.

Developing and Using a Personal Network of Contacts

Exploring the vast world of career and job options can be a daunting task for one individual to accomplish all alone. A much easier, more efficient, and more effective method would be to enlist the help of a personal network of contacts. Ask anyone how many people they have in their personal network of contacts, and they will probably respond "about fifteen or twenty." But in reality, each of us has dozens—even hundreds—of contacts who are as close as the telephone. Table 15 gives you an idea of the categories that these contacts fall into. These people all know your clients and some of them know their skills and interests. And clients have many hundreds of individuals in their potential network—that is, individuals that members of their current network can refer them to.

Table 16   Guidelines for Effective Networking—Level One

- Make a list of everyone you know.
- Find and write down their telephone numbers.
- Call each one and tell them that you are considering a job or career change and that you are seeking advice.
- Ask the contact what jobs, careers, or organizations he or she thinks you would best fit into.
- Ask for the opportunity to meet with the contact in person, if appropriate.
- Ask the contact to refer you to two new contacts who might have information.
- Thank the contact and offer to keep him or her posted on your progress (be sure to follow up on this).
- Make a record of when you talked, what advice was given, names and phone numbers of the referrals that were given, and some personal interest or hobby that the contact has.

Table 16 lists some guidelines for making initial networking contacts.

After clients have completed the first level of networking, they are ready to move on to the second level. Some guidelines are shown in table 17.

Some rules of thumb to remember when talking with a member of a personal network are shown in table 18.

Managing a Contact Network

A network can continue to produce results if managed properly. Educational experiments have shown that our memories for information and people decline rapidly from the time learned to about day 26 and then drops off completely. Consequently, contacts need to be renewed every month or two.

It is important to set up a system that you can use to actively manage a network. The people in a network are important. Each has taken the time to talk with the employee and many have given advice and referrals. In the implementation phase, some will be key in referring employees to actual jobs. Managing this network

Table 17   Guidelines for Effective Networking—Level Two

- Incorporate each reference into your network contact system (card file, three-ring binder, yellow tablet, or computer system).
- Call each new referral and introduce yourself, referring to your mutual friend or peer.
- Indicate that you are exploring, and ask the contact for information about the job, career, industry, or company that they represent.
- Ask for the opportunity (where practical) to meet face-to-face.
- Thank the person for the information that he or she has provided, and ask for the names of two referrals who can give you even more information about the job, career, industry, or organization.
- Again, tell the contact that you will keep him or her posted on your progress.
- As in level one, make a record of when you talked, what advice was given, names and phone numbers of referrals that were given, and some personal interest or hobby the contact has.

Table 18   Networking Dos and Don'ts

- When you are not sure if you should include a specific individual in your network, include him or her.
- Ask the contact for only that which he or she has in their power to give you.
- Do not ask for a job, unless the person has one to offer.
- Only ask questions that can't be answered no.
- At the end of an interview, ask what other advice the person would like to give you.

---

means making sure that each member is contacted every month or two to bring them up to date on the employee's progress. It also means doing something positive for the contact. In the next section, I deal with thank you notes. In addition, the employee could think about giving an inexpensive but personal gift to those who have offered their help.

Let me share an example of a thank you gift that I received last year. A young science teacher visited me in my office last year asking for advice on how to approach colleges for a job. While he was in my office, he noticed that I have a screen saver on my computer

Dear Mr. Jones:

Thank your for taking your valuable time to review my résumé and give me advice on potential career options.

Sincerely,

John Career-Changer

Figure 23 A Traditional Thank You Note

that showed Gary Larson's Far Side cartoons. Two or three weeks later I received a nice thank you note from the teacher with a newspaper clipping about Gary Larson. What this small but personal gesture said to me was that he was not just focused on what I could do for him, but on what he could do for me.

Thank You Notes

In the course of a career development or job search process, there are two phases at which many experts suggest showing appreciation to contacts with thank you notes: (a) during the exploration phase, when using contacts to gather information about potential options; and (b) during the job search implementation phase, when using contacts to obtain referrals to potential employment situations. I hold the opinion that the individual should avoid the traditional thank you notes, such as the one shown in figure 23.

While the traditional thank you note is a polite and appropriate gesture, it can be very impersonal. You could send the same note by just changing the name of the recipient to almost any contact, and contacts will recognize this. In figure 24, I have reproduced a more personal and specific thank you note. You can see that this note is specific to the contact. It was designed not only to thank him for his assistance but also to remind him specifically of what he did to help. It also implies that he will hear from the writer again.

Dear Mr. Jones,

Thanks for meeting with me last month and reviewing my résumé. I particularly appreciate your referring me to Neil Anderson at Ajax Corporation and Alice Steel with the Department of Commerce. Neil was very helpful in giving me an in-depth picture of Ajax. Although Ajax has no openings in my area at this time, I intend to check back with Neil periodically.

My contact with Alice Steel was even more productive. Alice was very generous with her time and was able to put me in touch with two organizations in Cleveland, where I have appointments next week.

Again, thanks for your valuable leads. I will keep you posted on the results.

Sincerely,

John Career-Changer

Figure 24   A Personal and Specific Thank You Note

As I indicated earlier, our memory of specific contacts often drops off rapidly after about four weeks. Consequently, I would suggest that the ideal time for the thank you note would be three or four weeks after the contact. This timing will also allow clients to report any tangible results of the referrals obtained from the contact.

What If the Same Referral Comes From Several Contacts?

While clients are in the exploration phase, it will not be uncommon for several contacts to refer them to the same individual. This will give you the opportunity for extra leverage in managing their network. First, if the same individual is mentioned by several contacts, he or she is probably an important person to talk with and incorporate into the network. When contacting this individual, it is advantageous to indicate that several people made the same referral, so he or she must be the right person to talk with. Furthermore, if the same name comes from five different contacts, your clientnow has a concrete reason to get back to each of the five contacts with a personal thank you note.

Exploring the Specifics of Career Options

The second part of the exploration phase of the career development process is to gather enough information about potential career or job options to be able to make an informed decision about which option is the most appropriate to focus on. The individual involved in a serious career development process is like the traveler standing at an intersection of several roads. Which road should I take? The traveler in too big a hurry will just speed down one road and have to accept the results. The more prudent strategy is to take an exploratory trip down each of the several roads to gather information on their characteristics and obtain a better view of where the roads lead. I call this active method of gathering important information about career options *field research*.

By field research, I do not mean "information interviews." When most busy people get a call from someone asking for an information interview, their reaction is that the caller doesn't want information—the caller wants a job. This situation has prompted me to suggest that we abandon the term *information interviewing* and substitute the term and concept of *field research*.

In Step 6 of this book, we included four major aspects of the individual that we wanted to assess in preparation for eventual career decision making: career values, career interests, motivated skills, and work style or management style. In the field research process, it is important to gather information on each of these four dimensions for each of the potential options that are under consideration.

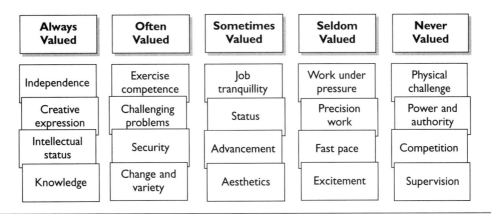

Always Valued	Often Valued	Sometimes Valued	Seldom Valued	Never Valued
Independence	Exercise competence	Job tranquillity	Work under pressure	Physical challenge
Creative expression	Challenging problems	Status	Precision work	Power and authority
Intellectual status	Security	Advancement	Fast pace	Competition
Knowledge	Change and variety	Aesthetics	Excitement	Supervision

Figure 25   Organizational Values

Determining the Career Values Associated With Options

The process of assessing the organization's career values should be conducted on each of the options that are being seriously considered. There are two basic methods for determining the career values needed in an organization or position. First, if clients have time for extensive research, they can read everything written about the organization, interview many individuals who are employed by the organization, and personally observe as much about the organization as possible. You can then work with the client to use the Career Values Card Sort from Appendix E, which was described in Step 6, and sort the values of the organizations into five categories as illustrated in the sample shown in figure 25.

A second method of determining the career values of the organization involves befriending an employee of the organization who knows the organization very well and could provide valuable insight. This individual could also be asked to use the Career Values Card Sort to help determine his or her view of the organization's career values.

Determining the Career Interests Associated With Options

Determining how career interests fit a specific job or career option is somewhat more complex than the process of using the Career Values cards to determine an organization's corporate values. When the employee has completed the Checklist of Career Interests in appendix B, he or she has identified 10 to 12 occupational titles that represented jobs that were appealing. Those were entered into section 1, item 2 on the Career Profile. At this point, it is necessary to examine the occupational titles and extract the one or two (or three) general themes that run through the selected job titles. For instance, if the employee has listed Broadcaster, Elected Public Official, Salesperson, Speech Pathologist, and Librarian as the occupations of interest, we can note that all deal with words and language. In addition, most require a college degree.

Once the employee has analyzed the occupational titles and extracted the themes, he or she can examine each option under consideration and determine just how well these themes fit the options.

Determining the Motivated Skills Associated With Options

When determining which motivated skills are associated with options, you are looking at a specific position or assignment rather than an organization in general. As with the career values assessment, you can have clients either research and observe the position or assignment, or they can select an individual who understands the requirements of the position very well and ask that individual to identify the skills necessary for accomplishing the tasks of the position. Using the Motivated Skills Card Sort from appendix F, which was described in Step 6, the individual selected can sort them into categories shown in the sample in figure 26.

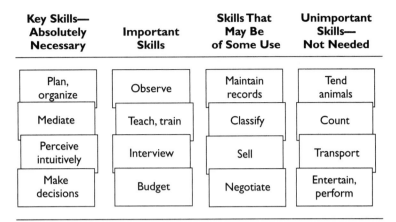

Key Skills— Absolutely Necessary	Important Skills	Skills That May Be of Some Use	Unimportant Skills— Not Needed
Plan, organize	Observe	Maintain records	Tend animals
Mediate	Teach, train	Classify	Count
Perceive intuitively	Interview	Sell	Transport
Make decisions	Budget	Negotiate	Entertain, perform

Figure 26   Skills Required for Success in the Position

Determining the Work Style or Management Style Associated With Options

A critical element of any position is the work style or management style that is most appropriate to successful work in the position. As with values, skills, and interests, the position in question can be researched and observed to determine which work style or styles are most appropriate or effective in the position. In addition, an individual who knows the position very well (may currently hold the position or manage or supervise individuals who hold the position) can be identified to complete the Work Style Survey from appendix C. Make sure the individual understands that he or she is to fill out the survey *for the position,* not the individual holding the position. The results should yield an "ideal workstyle" for the position, similar to that presented in table 19.

When the four elements or dimensions of values, interests, skills, and work style that are associated with each of the potential options have been determined, the individual is then ready to list at least five jobs or careers that he or she wants to explore on

Table 19 Work Styles Associated With a Specific Position

Ideal or Best Work Style	Appropriate Work Style	Acceptable Work Style	Inappropriate Work Style
Analytical	Action	Creative	Emotional

section 2 of the Employee Career Profile. The employee should be reminded to focus only on appropriate and realistic jobs or careers at this point.

Participate in Employee's Goal Setting and Planning

One of the reasons many people have difficulty attaining career or job satisfaction is the lack of a clear vision of a very specific goal. In this step, we will focus on two key questions for the individual engaged in career development:

- What is my specific career goal?
- Why is this the best goal for me?

What Is the Specific Career Goal?

Many of us have seen résumés that contain a "career objective" that goes somewhat like this: "to obtain a challenging position that offers an opportunity for growth in a dynamic organization." Clearly, we have very little idea of exactly what this individual's career or job objective is. Computer programmer? Sales manager?

Janitor? Physician? This career objective would fit any position. My rule of thumb for résumés is to either have a very short and specific objective (such as "systems analyst" or "assistant retail store manager") or to leave out the category of objective all together.

The following anecdote exemplifies how specific the objective needs to be. Let us assume that there are five stacks of résumés sitting on the desk in an employment manager's office. Each stack is in a tray marked with the specific job opening that the résumé was directed toward. Now, let us assume that the janitor (possibly not an English speaker) accidentally knocks all of the résumés onto the floor. I believe that the objective at the top of each résumé needs to be so simple and clear that the janitor could pick them up and put them back into the correct tray.

The emphasis on a specific goal is not intended to put the employee into a box or to tie the employee to a specific goal for eternity. Rather, this emphasis on specific goals is to teach the employee the process of specifying and articulating clear and specific goals.

Sharing the Task With Others

An effective method of focusing on an appropriate job or career goal is to enlist the help of other individuals. A career focus group activity could be part of a career development workshop. The individual developing the career goal can ask two or more fellow workshop participants to listen to a presentation of the individual's attributes and options and render their views on how appropriate one or more of the career options are. Table 20 presents an outline of a group focus session.

Using this group process, the individual can receive feedback on how much each attribute fits the requirements of each option. He or she can then begin to develop a focus on the specific option that fits the best.

Building a Career Development Program

Table 20   Guidelines for Conducting a Career Focus Group Activity

Presentation by the Career Decision Maker

"My career values are. . . ."

"My motivated skills are. . . ."

"My occupational interest themes are. . . ."

"My work style or management style is. . . ."

"My career options are. . . . "

Response by Individual Group Members

"Your career values seem consistent with. . . ."

"Your motivated skills would be necessary in. . . ."

"Your occupational interests seem consistent with. . . ."

"Your work style or management style seems to match. . . ."

Using a Spreadsheet to Sharpen the Focus

If the individual does not have access to a group for support, he or she can use a spreadsheet (manual or computerized) to develop a career focus. The individual can list the options from the exploration section of his or her Employee Career Profile across the top of the spreadsheet along the horizontal axis. The individual's attributes (career values, career interests, motivated skills, and work or management style) can then be listed down the vertical axis on the spreadsheet. A typical spreadsheet is shown in figure 27.

The individual can use any type of rating system when comparing each attribute with each option. A typical rating system is outlined in table 21.

Using either the group or the spreadsheet process described above, the individual can develop a clear vision and sharp focus on an appropriate career goal that best represents a match with his or her values, interests, skills, and work style. This information is then recorded in section III of the Employee Career Profile.

At this initial stage, we are not preoccupied with how realistic the career goal is—only that the goal be clearly specified and

Range of Career Options

Individual Attributes	Realtor	Insurance Agent	Sales Manager	Teacher/ Trainer	Human Resources Administrator
Career Values					
Career Interests					
Motivated Skills					
Work or Management Style					

Figure 27   Sample Spreadsheet for Developing a Career Focus

Table 21   Key for Rating Attribute-Option Fit

++	=	Excellent fit
+	=	Good fit
—	=	Complete misfit
-	=	Some misfit
0	=	Not applicable or irrelevant
?	=	Need more information on how the option and attribute fit

articulated. It is often best to resist placing an emphasis on being realistic, as that might extinguish or dampen some of the individual's creativity. When helping the client to decide on a specific career or job goal, the career coach could consider Carl Rogers' book on "unconditional positive regard" for the client and his or her aspirations. At the next phase, however, the "why" phase, we need to turn to such teachers as Albert Ellis and his bent toward reality.

Why Is This the Best Goal?

In order to determine if the selected option is the best option for the individual, the most effective method is to challenge the employee to lay out clear and compelling evidence that this is the most appropriate option. By evidence, I mean specifying which of the individual's career values are congruent with the selected option, which of the individual's career interests are consistent with the selected option, which of the individual's motivated skills are necessary to successfully accomplish tasks central to the selected option, and how compatible the individual's work or management style is with the style requirements of the selected option. Table 22 illustrates one employee's answer to the "why" question.

It is highly recommended that each individual involved in career planning and development go through the process of justifying or

Table 22 Why Is This Job the Best Option for Me?

Option chosen:	Writer of technical manuals
Career values:	Exercise competence, precision work, creativity, job tranquility
Career interests:	Words, creativity
Motivated skills:	Design, analyze, write, classify, proofread, and edit
Work or management style:	Analytical, expressive

proving that the option they have selected as a career focus is the best choice for him or her. If the career coach is working with just one client, this process can involve the employee attempting to convince the coach that this is the best option. In a group setting, this step can be even more powerful. The career coach can ask the client to consider the group as a jury and to present clear evidence to them to prove that the chosen option is the best possible option. If the employee can convince the coach or the group of the appropriateness of the option, it just might be the right option to pursue. On the other hand, if the employee fails to convince either the coach or the group of the appropriateness of the chosen option, the employee can move to a second (or backup) option. It is better to try and fail in the safe presence of the coach or support group than to fail in an interview for a real job.

Coach Employee in Implementing the Career Strategy

All of the work and energy that the individual employee has devoted to the previous three steps of career development (assessment, exploration, and goal setting) would be for naught without culminating in the implementation of a career strategy plan. The major elements of a career strategy plan can be summarized by these key questions:

- *How* will I get to the goal?
- *When* will each step in my plan occur?
- *Who* else will or should be involved in my plan?

How Will I Get to the Goal?

This "how" question relates to exactly what behaviors the employee will engage in to reach the goal. At this point, we do not want

**Table 23 Sample Questions the Coach Can Ask
to Get the Employee to Be Specific**

Q: What is the very next thing that you will do in order to get to your goal of auto mechanic?

A: I will take a course in auto mechanics.

Q: Where will you take the course?

A: I don't know. Maybe at the community college.

Q: How will you decide on what school to go to?

A: I guess I will look at the college catalogs.

Q: After you look at the college catalogs, what will you do next?

A: I guess I will visit several of the colleges.

Q: Do you know what you will ask at each college?

A: No, I have not thought about it.

Q: Do you think you should write up a list of questions?

A: Yes, that's a good idea. I'll make a list of questions.

---

to know what the organization or the supervisor or manager will do to help the employee attain the goal. Many employees have a tendency to be too general at this phase. Table 23 shows some sample questions the career coach can ask the employee in order to help him or her move from the general to the specific.

When Will Each Step in My Plan Occur?

This "when" question relates to exactly when each goal-directed behavior will occur. It is not sufficient that the employee specify each step towards the career goal. To ensure movement, the individual should set out a specific and detailed time frame. Table 24 lists some sample questions to help the employee establish a specific time line.

Having the employee specify the exact times that he or she will engage in a goal-directed behavior will be most effective if it is written down. Consequently, I usually ask the employees to bring their

Table 24 Sample Questions the Coach Can Ask to Elicit a Specific Time Line

Q: When will you look at the college catalogs?

A: I'll do it next week.

Q: What day next week?

A: Next Tuesday.

Q: What time next Tuesday?

A: In the afternoon.

Q: What exact time next Tuesday afternoon?

A: At the end of the day, at 4:30 P.M.

daily planners with them to each coaching session. I ask them to list each planned action on the appropriate page in the planner. Sometimes I even ask them to use an ink pen rather than a pencil. I make it very clear to the employees that my insistence on such detailed recording of the plan is not to overwork them, but to increase the probability that they will be successful.

Who Else Will or Should Be Involved in My Plan?

This "who" question is often necessary in order to encourage the employee to involve others in the career strategy plan. There are three classes of people involved in an individual's career planning process: people whom the plan will affect, people who can be of assistance, and people who fit both categories. One person who fits both categories is the employee's direct supervisor. The supervisor is (or should be) an important stakeholder in an employee's career planning. Whether the employee wants to stay within the department or move out to another department (or company), the employee's decision will directly affect the supervisor. The supervisor should be advised of the employee's goals and plans, and ideally, serve as an advisor and coach to assist in the employee's career development. Others who can be affected by the employee's career planning include the spouse and other family members. If the employee decides to attend night school as part of a career development plan how will the spouse feel? Both spouse and supervisor can be of assistance to the employee in the career planning process. Often, it is the spouse's psychological support that can spell the difference between success and failure of even the best laid career plans. The supervisor can be key to identifying and opening career development doors for the employee. Managers who truly want to develop their employees are more than willing to assist them in their career development—even when it means losing a valued employee. Table 15, *Categories of People Who Could Be Starting Contacts for a Potential Network*, in Step 7 lists many other people who can be of assistance in helping employees implement their career plans. The names of these individuals should be entered at the end of section 4 of the Employee Career Profile.

Employee
Career Profile

Section I.   CAREER ASSESSMENT

1. List your six to eight most important career values.

   _____

   _____

   _____

   _____

2. List your six to eight strongest career interests.

   _____

   _____

   _____

   _____

3. List your six to eight most highly motivated skills.

   _____

   _____

   _____

   _____

4. List your highest one or two work or management styles.

_____

_____

Section II. CAREER EXPLORATION

1. List at least five jobs or careers that you can pursue.

_____

_____

_____

_____

_____

Section III. CAREER FOCUS—YOUR GOAL

1. List the option from section II that fits you the best.
   What is your goal?

_____

_____

2. Why is this the best goal for you? List evidence (skills, values, etc.) that show the above goal is the very best possible goal for you.

_____

_____

_____

_____

_____

_____

_____

_____

_____

_____

_____

Section IV. CAREER STRATEGY AND IMPLEMENTATION PLAN

1. How will you get to your goal? What specific behavior will you engage in to attain your goal? Be clear and specific about what you will do.

_____

_____

_____

_____

_____

_____

_____

_____

_____

2. When will each step to your career goal occur?

_____

_____

_____

_____

_____

_____

_____

3. Who will be affected by your plan? Who can help you in your plan?

_____

_____

_____

_____

_____

_____

Appendix B

Checklist of Career Interests

	Definitely Interested	Probably Interested	Indifferent	Probably Not Interested	Definitely Not Interested
Realtor	❑	❑	❑	❑	❑
Physical education teacher	❑	❑	❑	❑	❑
Physicist	❑	❑	❑	❑	❑
Landscape gardener	❑	❑	❑	❑	❑
Airline ticket agent	❑	❑	❑	❑	❑
Juvenile parole officer	❑	❑	❑	❑	❑
Telephone operator	❑	❑	❑	❑	❑
Public administrator	❑	❑	❑	❑	❑
Bookkeeper	❑	❑	❑	❑	❑
Recreation leader	❑	❑	❑	❑	❑

	Definitely Interested	Probably Interested	Indifferent	Probably Not Interested	Definitely Not Interested
Farmer	❑	❑	❑	❑	❑
Insurance agent	❑	❑	❑	❑	❑
Sales manager	❑	❑	❑	❑	❑
Pharmacist	❑	❑	❑	❑	❑
Social worker	❑	❑	❑	❑	❑
Entertainer	❑	❑	❑	❑	❑
Interior designer	❑	❑	❑	❑	❑
Instrument assembler	❑	❑	❑	❑	❑
Waiter/waitress	❑	❑	❑	❑	❑
Medical lab technician	❑	❑	❑	❑	❑
Department store manager	❑	❑	❑	❑	❑
Purchasing agent	❑	❑	❑	❑	❑
Architect	❑	❑	❑	❑	❑
Minister	❑	❑	❑	❑	❑
Guidance counselor	❑	❑	❑	❑	❑
Clothes designer	❑	❑	❑	❑	❑
Dental hygienist	❑	❑	❑	❑	❑
Forest ranger	❑	❑	❑	❑	❑
Food service manager	❑	❑	❑	❑	❑
Artist	❑	❑	❑	❑	❑
Costume designer	❑	❑	❑	❑	❑

	Definitely Interested	Probably Interested	Indifferent	Probably Not Interested	Definitely Not Interested
Child-care assistant	❏	❏	❏	❏	❏
Illustrator	❏	❏	❏	❏	❏
Psychologist	❏	❏	❏	❏	❏
Veterinarian	❏	❏	❏	❏	❏
Executive housekeeper	❏	❏	❏	❏	❏
Banker	❏	❏	❏	❏	❏
Optometrist	❏	❏	❏	❏	❏
Wholesaler	❏	❏	❏	❏	❏
Buyer, merchandise	❏	❏	❏	❏	❏
Dental assistant	❏	❏	❏	❏	❏
Rancher	❏	❏	❏	❏	❏
Dentist	❏	❏	❏	❏	❏
Court reporter	❏	❏	❏	❏	❏
Accountant	❏	❏	❏	❏	❏
Innkeeper	❏	❏	❏	❏	❏
Dietitian	❏	❏	❏	❏	❏
School superintendent	❏	❏	❏	❏	❏
Chamber of commerce executive	❏	❏	❏	❏	❏
Social science teacher	❏	❏	❏	❏	❏
Chemist	❏	❏	❏	❏	❏
Elementary teacher	❏	❏	❏	❏	❏

	Definitely Interested	Probably Interested	Indifferent	Probably Not Interested	Definitely Not Interested
Florist	❏	❏	❏	❏	❏
Mathematician	❏	❏	❏	❏	❏
Language teacher	❏	❏	❏	❏	❏
Fashion model	❏	❏	❏	❏	❏
Office clerk	❏	❏	❏	❏	❏
Computer operator	❏	❏	❏	❏	❏
Advertising executive	❏	❏	❏	❏	❏
Physician	❏	❏	❏	❏	❏
Mail carrier	❏	❏	❏	❏	❏
Chiropractor	❏	❏	❏	❏	❏
Math-science teacher	❏	❏	❏	❏	❏
Physical therapist	❏	❏	❏	❏	❏
Military officer	❏	❏	❏	❏	❏
Labor arbitrator	❏	❏	❏	❏	❏
Dancer	❏	❏	❏	❏	❏
Technical writer	❏	❏	❏	❏	❏
Pilot	❏	❏	❏	❏	❏
Police officer	❏	❏	❏	❏	❏
Economist	❏	❏	❏	❏	❏
Receptionist	❏	❏	❏	❏	❏
Retailer	❏	❏	❏	❏	❏
Public relations director	❏	❏	❏	❏	❏

	Definitely Interested	Probably Interested	Indifferent	Probably Not Interested	Definitely Not Interested
Carpenter	❏	❏	❏	❏	❏
Computer salesperson	❏	❏	❏	❏	❏
Optician	❏	❏	❏	❏	❏
Machinist	❏	❏	❏	❏	❏
Office manager	❏	❏	❏	❏	❏
Musician	❏	❏	❏	❏	❏
Social scientist	❏	❏	❏	❏	❏
Secretary	❏	❏	❏	❏	❏
Keypunch operator	❏	❏	❏	❏	❏
Photographer	❏	❏	❏	❏	❏
Printer	❏	❏	❏	❏	❏
Nurse	❏	❏	❏	❏	❏
Production manager	❏	❏	❏	❏	❏
Engineer	❏	❏	❏	❏	❏
Employment manager	❏	❏	❏	❏	❏
College professor	❏	❏	❏	❏	❏
Proofreader	❏	❏	❏	❏	❏
Statistician	❏	❏	❏	❏	❏
Electronics technician	❏	❏	❏	❏	❏
Television announcer	❏	❏	❏	❏	❏
Personnel director	❏	❏	❏	❏	❏

	Definitely Interested	Probably Interested	Indifferent	Probably Not Interested	Definitely Not Interested
Mechanic	❏	❏	❏	❏	❏
County welfare worker	❏	❏	❏	❏	❏
State legislator	❏	❏	❏	❏	❏
Newspaper reporter	❏	❏	❏	❏	❏
Stockbroker	❏	❏	❏	❏	❏
Politician	❏	❏	❏	❏	❏
Electrician	❏	❏	❏	❏	❏
Truck driver	❏	❏	❏	❏	❏
Business education teacher	❏	❏	❏	❏	❏
Author	❏	❏	❏	❏	❏
Librarian	❏	❏	❏	❏	❏
Computer programmer	❏	❏	❏	❏	❏
Travel agent	❏	❏	❏	❏	❏
Credit manager	❏	❏	❏	❏	❏
Beautician	❏	❏	❏	❏	❏
Lawyer	❏	❏	❏	❏	❏
Operating room technician	❏	❏	❏	❏	❏
Building contractor	❏	❏	❏	❏	❏

Work Style Survey

Directions

In each of the twelve questions on the next page, there are four descriptive words or terms. For each item, you are asked to choose the word that most people who know you would say accurately described you. Give that word 4 points and write the number next to the word. On the same question, choose the word or term that is the next best in describing you and give that word 3 points. Give the word that is next best at describing you 2 points. Finally, give the word that is least accurate in describing you 1 point. Follow the same process for all twelve questions.

Example

1. Logical   **3**   Emotional   **1**   Practical   **4**   Intellectual   **2**

When you have completed all twelve questions, add the points for each row. Then plot your Work Style score on the next page.

Work Style Survey

	A	B	C	D
1.	Logical	Emotional	Practical	Intellectual
2.	Systematic	Stimulating	Realistic	Creative
3.	Careful	Responsive	Quick	Ingenious
4.	Planful	Empathetic	Immediate	Future thinker
5.	Calm	Feeling	Pragmatic	Big picture
6.	Precise	Sociable	Here and now	Unique
7.	Fact oriented	People person	Doer	Conceptualizer
8.	Uses data	Uses charm	Gets results	Generate ideas
9.	Good analyzer	Good listener	Type A	Original thinker
10.	Info person	Warm	Energetic	Global thinker
11.	Organized	Approachable	Resourceful	Bright
12.	Competent	Nonthreatening	Hands-on	Innovator

Row A	**Analytical**—detailed and logical	Points_____
Row B	**Emotional**—sensitive and friendly	Points_____
Row C	**Action**—multitasked and quick	Points_____
Row D	**Creative**—big-picture and future-oriented	Points_____

Resources for Career Coaches

Credentials

Career coaches in organizations should become familiar with the range of credentialing available for practitioners. Three widely accepted credentialing processes exist.

National Certified Career Counselor (NCCC)

The longest established credential is the National Certified Career Counselor (NCCC) credential offered by the National Board for Certified Counselors. This credential is for counselors who possess a master's degree (48 semester units or 72 quarter units) in counseling or counseling psychology, have completed 3,000 postgraduate hours of supervised experience in counseling, have completed course work in career theory and assessment, and have passed two national examinations (a generic counseling exam and a specialty exam for career counseling). Information about the National

Certified Career Counselor (NCCC) credential and application form are available from:

National Board for Certified Counselors
3-D Terrace Way
Greensboro, NC 49008
Tel: (910) 547-0607
Fax: (910) 547-0017

Member of the Outplacement Institute (MOI)

In 1994, two organizations, the International Association of Career Management Professionals (IACMP) and the Association of Outplacement Consulting Firms International (AOCFI) formed the Outplacement Institute to certify the competency of outplacement consultants. To become a Member of the Outplacement Institute (MOI), an individual must document at least ten years of professional/administrative work experience, at least five years of work experience as an outplacement consultant, and demonstrate competency in the following areas:

- Consulting with client companies
- Conducting or supervising individual and group coaching or counseling
- Administering and interpreting career assessment instruments
- Knowledge of the job search process
- Knowledge of the career planning and development process

Competence and experience in the above areas is determined by the documented portfolio that each candidate for membership in the MOI develops and turns in to a sponsoring mentor, who must be a Fellow of the Outplacement Institute.

A higher level of certification is the designation of Fellow of the Outplacement Institute (FOI), which requires 15 years of professional experience and ten years of outplacement experience, as well as documented competence in the five areas listed above. Both member and fellow credentials require sponsorship by a fellow of the Outplacement Institute and the completion of a portfolio that documents the experience and competence of the applicant.

For information, or membership procedures, contact:

International Association of Career
Management Professionals (IACMP)
P.O. Box 1484
Pacifica, CA 94044-6484
Tel: (415) 359-6911
Fax (415) 359-3089

The Outplacement Institute
P.O. Box 150759
San Rafael, CA 94915
Tel: (415) 459-2235
Fax: (415) 459-6298

Association of Outplacement Consulting Firms International (AOCFI)
1200 19th St. NW, Suite 300
Washington, DC 20036-2422
Tel: (202) 857-1185
Fax: (202) 857-1115

Certified Job and Career Transition Coach (CJCTC)

The Certified Job and Career Transition Coach is the newest of the three credentials. This international credential was established in November 1994 by the Career Planning and Adult Development Network. The Job and Career Transition Coach credential involves the completion of a twenty-one-hour, in-depth career coaching workshop where applicants' competencies and knowledge in applying specific career coaching behaviors are evaluated. Successful coaches demonstrate their knowledge and expertise in the following areas:

- Short-term job transitions and long-term career transition dynamics
- Techniques for ventilation and dealing with the emotions associated with voluntary and involuntary transitions

- Career assessment instruments and exercises
- Career and job exploration techniques
- Field research methods
- Career and job goal setting
- Career search planning
- Job search strategy planning
- Résumés and vitae
- Network development and maintenance
- Interview techniques
- Salary negotiation
- Job offer evaluation

Information about the Job and Career Transition Coach certification process can be obtained from:

Career Planning and Adult Development Network
4965 Sierra Road
San Jose, CA 95132
Tel: (408) 559-4946
Fax: (408) 559-8211

Professional Associations

One of the most effective methods of staying up to date on career coaching, career counseling, and job search developments is to participate in one or more professional associations. Some appropriate associations are:

American Society for Training and Development (ASTD)
1640 King Street
Alexandria, VA 22313-2043 USA
Tel: (703) 683-8100
Fax: (703) 683-8103

Many ASTD members are trainers within organizations or external training consultants. There is a career development professional practice area within ASTD.

Career Planning and Adult Development Network
(NETWORK)
4965 Sierra Road
San Jose, CA 95132
Tel: (408) 559-4946
Fax: (408) 559-8211

The NETWORK publishes a monthly newsletter and a quarterly journal for professionals who work with adults in job or career transition. In addition to administering the Job and Career Transition Coach Certification program, the NETWORK sponsors the California Career Conference and its companion International Career Development Symposium that attracts over 1,000 career development professionals from throughout the world to California each November.

International Association of
Career Management Professionals (IACMP)
P.O. Box 1484
Pacifica, CA 94044-6484
Tel: (415) 359-6911
Fax (415) 359-3089

IACMP members work in corporate outplacement, organizational career development, and private practice. There are local chapters throughout the world.

National Association for Job Search Training (NAJST)
Tel: (606) 257-6576
Fax: (606) 323-1085

Members of NAJST are job search trainers and counselors who work in colleges, universities, government agencies, private social service agencies, and private training consultation practice.

National Career Development Association (NCDA)
5999 Stevenson Avenue
Alexandria, VA 22304-3300
Tel: (800) 347-6647 ext. 309
Fax: (703) 751-2294

Members of this division of the American Counseling Association are career counselors who work in education, government, public agencies, and private practice.

National Employment Counseling Association (NECA)
Tel: (703) 823-9800
Fax: (703) 823-0252

Members of this division of the American Counseling Association are professionals who work in employment and training settings.

Society for Human Resource Management (SHRM)
606 N. Washington Street
Alexandria, VA 22314
Tel: (703) 548-3440
Fax: (703) 836-0367

Members of SHRM work in human resource and personnel departments in public and private organizations around the world.

Professional Conferences

Conferences with speakers and workshops of interest to career coaches include:

National Career Development Association Conference

Held in January of every other year in a southern U.S. location, this conference attracts 700 to 800 participants.

National Consultation on Career Development (NATCON)

Held every January in Ottawa, Ontario, Canada, this conference draws over 1,000 career professionals from across Canada.

California Career Conference (CCC)

Held in late October or early November of each year in California, this conference draws over 1,000 career professionals from throughout North America, Europe, and Australia.

International Association for Career Management
Professionals (IACMP) Conference

An international conference is held in North America every
spring and a European conference is held in Europe every fall.

National Association for Job Search Training
(NAJST) Conference

A national conference is held every year in March or April in
the U.S.

Training Seminars

Two training seminars that provide training in career development
and job search techniques are:

Richard Bolles' Two-week Residential Seminar
on Work/Life Planning

This two-week workshop is held in August of each year in Bend,
Oregon. Instructors include Richard Bolles, Daniel Porot, and
David Swanson.

What Color Is Your Parachute?
P.O. Box 379 Walnut Creek, CA 94597
Tel: (510) 837-3002
Fax: (510) 837-5120

Job and Career Transition Coach Certification Seminar
This three-day seminar is held several times per year in North
America, Europe, and Australia. The focus is developing skills to
guide adults through short-term job transitions and long-term
career transitions. The instructor is Richard L. Knowdell. For
information, contact:

Career Planning and Adult Development Network
(NETWORK)
4965 Sierra Road
San Jose, CA 95132
Tel: (408) 559-4945
Fax: (408) 559-8211

Training and Testing Materials

Career Research & Testing, Inc.
2005 Hamilton Avenue, Suite 250
San Jose, CA 95125
Tel: (800) 888-4945
Fax: (408) 559-8211

Career Systems
900 James Avenue
Scranton, PA 18510
Tel: (800) 283-8839
Fax: (717) 346-8606

Center for Worklife Counseling
P. O. Box 407
Spit Junction, NSW 2088
AUSTRALIA
Tel: 011 61 2 9968.1588
Fax: 011 61 2 9968.1655

Communication Consultants
20 Beverly Road
West Hartford Road
West Hartford, CT 06119
Tel: (203) 233-1396
Fax: (203) 232-1321

CPP, Inc.
1055 Joaquin Road, 2nd Floor
Mountain View, CA 94043
Tel: (800) 624-1765
Fax: (650) 969-8608

Consulting Resource Group
International
368-200 West Third Street
Sumas, WA 98295-8000
Tel: (604) 852-0566
Fax: (604) 850-3003

Drake Beam Morin, Inc.
100 Park Avenue
New York, NY 10017
Tel: (800) 345-5627
Fax: (212) 972-2120

JIST Works, Inc.
720 North Park Avenue
Indianapolis, IN 46202-3431
Tel: (800) 648-5478
Fax: (317) 264-3709

Psychological Assessment
Resources
P. O. Box 998
Odessa, FL 33556
Tel: (800) 331-8378
Fax: (800) 727-9329

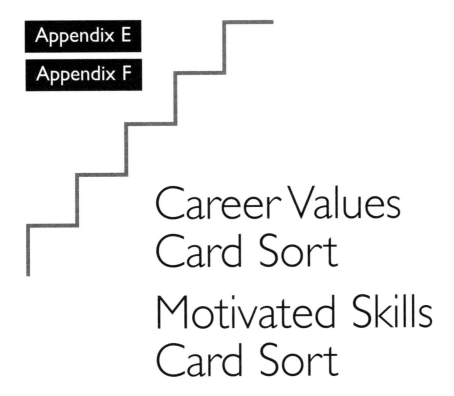

Career Values Card Sort

Motivated Skills Card Sort

Directions

Appendices E and F contain two assessment instruments that readers may use to prioritize their career values and identify their motivated skills. The pages containing these card sort instruments (located at the back of this book) have been perforated along the spine to allow the reader to remove the sheets and cut each card sort into a deck of cards. Cut the cards carefully along the dotted lines and follow the directions for using them in Step 6 (pages 61–76). You may use each deck as many times as you would like and with as many employees as necessary.

Index